Our Churches Tell the Story

A VISUAL SURVEY OF THE BIBLE

Photography and Editing by Denise Z. Park

Scripture taken from the
New King James Version.
Copyright (c) 1982 by
Thomas Nelson, Inc.
Used by permission.

First published in the
United States by:
Evergreen Press
of Brainerd, LLC.
P.O. Box 465
201 West Laurel Street
Brainerd, MN 56401
(218) 828-6424
www.evergreenpress.org

Photography / Editing:
Denise Z. Park

Project Management:
Beth Hautala

Associate Editor:
Jodi Schwen

Cover and Interior Design:
Aaron Hautala

Color / Production
Management:
Bryan Petersen

ISBN 0-9661599-8-5
Printed in the United States of America
FIRST EDITION

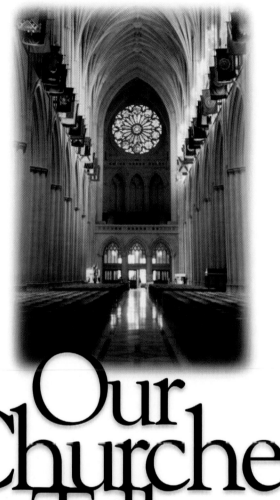

THE WASHINGTON
NATIONAL
CATHEDRAL,
Washington, D.C.

Our Churches Tell *the* Story

A VISUAL SURVEY OF THE BIBLE

Photography and Editing by Denise Z. Park

ST. ANDREW'S
CATHOLIC CHURCH
Roanoke, VA

Dedication
of this book is made to our
Father God with heartfelt gratitude.

He is forever reaching into our lives, expressing His care, His

love, and His creativity through His children. He did so with me

as He challenged and stretched me to accomplish something that

would help others to feel, through visual experience, His awesome

presence and goodness expressed in various forms of art found in

churches, where His people seek to honor and glorify Him. I

truly hope that my efforts in being obedient, open to Him,

and my attitude of delight in doing this project,

can be my gift of love back to

Him.

First in gratitude, I wish to thank my husband, Steve, for his support. I am thankful for his major coaching skills, for teaching me to use the computer, and for rescuing me from many a computer crisis. Secondly, I cannot omit thanking Chip Borkenhagen for authorizing Beth and Aaron Hautala, as editor and artist, to do the stellar job they have done, using their gifts and dedication to make this special book a reality. I am sure that they will be blessed. In my personal life, I am grateful for two women who came into my life during the '80s to bring me across that bridge from death to life—the death of my past to hope for the future. Paula Brownlee, a past president of my college, obeyed the call of God, and for a time, became to me a life preserver in my ocean of despair. Martha Glennan became a dear friend. Often when life is most difficult, God places people in our lives who have had a more challenging journey. My emotional disabilities began to heal as I observed how beautifully Martha handled severe physical disabilities as a challenge; she did so with great faith with no trace of bitterness. I give my Father great thanks for these two women. Lastly, I give thanks to all the churches, the dear pastors, and the "sheep" who so graciously let me feast on the treasures that follow.

—D.Z.P

"If anyone hears My voice and opens the door, I will come in to him and dine with him, and he with Me."

REVELATION 3:20B

ACKNOWLEDGMENTS

he power of Christian symbolism has been in evidence since early believers first identified themselves to one another by tracing the form of a fish in the sand. The relationship of the first letters of the Greek *ikthous* (fish) clearly became a meaningful statement declaring *Jesus Christ, Son of God*.

As we crest the second millennium since the Savior came and launch the third in anticipation of His return, I welcome every medium possible that commits to spreading "the truth as it is in Jesus."

This splendid presentation of the artistry of the ages is a marvelous means for achieving yet another means of communicating God's Word as it was given to us—both in print and in person—in the Bible, and in His Son, Jesus Christ.

May that eternal message not only become clearer through the brightness of these images, but may the Light of the World shine ever more brilliantly in each heart that opens before the Sonlight contained here.

JACK W. HAYFORD / PASTOR, THE CHURCH ON THE WAY
President, The King's Seminary / *Van Nuys, CA*

F O R W A R D

*i*n the past, especially in Europe, stained glass windows in the cathedrals have been a means of instruction visually exemplifying the Bible. Because I am a visual person, I have found that color and shapes within a picture make more of an impression on my mind than mere words. Perhaps this is the reason God called me to write this book. It has been an immense teaching tool for me, and I believe there must be many, who like me, share a visual orientation. May this book be as much a gift to them from the Lord as it has been to me—not only to encourage, comfort, and teach, but to help them become more intimately acquainted with our wonderful Creator God, His son Jesus, and the Holy Spirit.

For much of my life, I tried to appease God because I was convinced He was strict and angry. I strived and cried, but this brought only frustration and anger toward myself and the world with which I could not cope. When I hit rock bottom, I reached out to others in the imperfect but beautiful body of Christ—His church. There I received the support of a caring family. During this time, God showed me the complete love of His Son, Jesus, who appeared to me at the point of death. I have never felt such love and acceptance. Later, after surrendering my life to God, I realized that life is much like a mosaic or stained glass window in the hands of a Great Craftsman and Artist. He had replaced the shattered pieces of my dreams and broken heart with His dreams and His heart. No longer do I see my God as a strict and angry Creator who intentionally causes suffering and trouble for those living in a world already filled with pain. Instead, He is a loving and caring Father who desires the best for me and for all of His children. I have learned that when I give Him first place in my life, my problems are much more open to His solutions, which are often unusual and unexpected. As I trust in Him, His flawless character, and unceasing love, I experience more and more of the abundant life He promised me. My life is not without challenges, but His Son, Jesus, is closer than any friend.

Too many people have no idea how profoundly the Bible can impact their lives. God delights to reveal Himself through His Holy WORD. He has sent the Holy Spirit to enable us to receive His unlimited treasures. As you travel with me through the pages that follow, I pray you will discover this God who cares deeply for you. May you be loved, instructed, and blessed.

—Denise Z. Park

All of the photographs are my own, except for the one on page 166. These images were captured with two automatic pocket cameras, a Pentax IQZoom 120, and a Minolta Freedom zoom 140X, using Kodak MAX 800, and Kodak Gold 200 speed film. The rest is God's light and direction. This window, located within a small church in Utah, gave me spiritual rest from the rigors of driving around the West, alone, on a 14,000 mile trip. It was here in 1998, that I received the idea or commission to begin a mini-pictorial version of the Bible, which took me a year to complete.

GRACE BAPTIST CHURCH
Washington, UT

ARTIST STATEMENT

The Story
SECTIONS

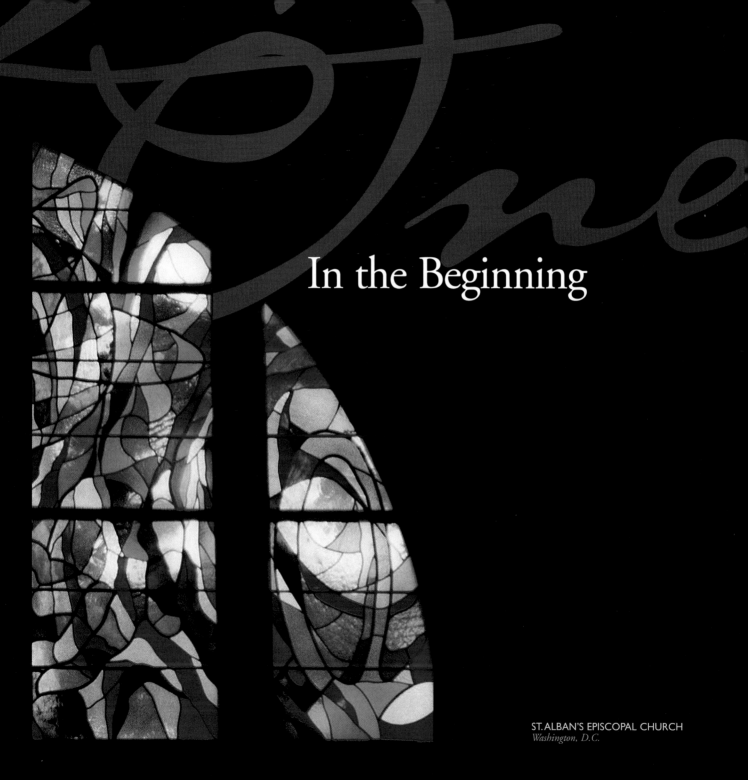

In the Beginning

ST. ALBAN'S EPISCOPAL CHURCH
Washington, D.C.

THE WASHINGTON
NATIONAL CATHEDRAL
Washington, D.C.

The moon rock, portrayed
in the upper part of this
window, was a gift from
the crew of Apollo 11, who
went to the moon in 1969.

IN THE BEGINNING, THE LORD GOD CREATED THE HEAVENS

GENESIS 1:1–5A, 16–18

I n the beginning God created the heavens and the earth. The earth was without form, and void; and darkness was on the face of the deep. And the Spirit of God was hovering over the face of the waters. Then God said, "Let there be light;" and there was light. And God saw the light, that it was good; and God divided the light from the darkness. God called the light Day, and the darkness He called Night. Then God made two great lights: the greater light to rule the day, and the lesser light to rule the night. He made the stars also. God set them in the firmament of the heavens to give light on the earth, and to rule over the day and over the night, and to divide the light from the darkness. And God saw that it was good.

EMMANUEL EPISCOPAL CHURCH,
Rapidan, VA

AND HE CREATED THE EARTH

GENESIS 1:9–12

Then God said, "Let the waters under the heavens be gathered together into one place, and let the dry land appear;" and it was so. And God called the dry land Earth, and the gathering together of the waters He called Seas. And God saw that it was good. Then God said, "Let the earth bring forth grass, the herb that yields seed, and the fruit tree that yields fruit according to its kind, whose seed is in itself, on the earth;" and it was so. And the earth brought forth grass, the herb that yields seed according to its kind, and the tree that yields fruit, whose seed is in itself according to its kind. And God saw that it was good.

GOD CREATED MAN

GENESIS 1:26A,
27–28A; 2:7, 18, 21–24

Then God said, "Let Us make man in Our image, according to Our likeness." So God created man in His own image . . . male and female He created them. Then God blessed them, and God said to them, "Be fruitful and multiply; fill the earth and subdue it." And the LORD God formed man of the dust of the ground, and breathed into his nostrils the breath of life; and man became a living being. And the LORD God said, "It is not good that man should be alone; I will make him a helper comparable to him." And the LORD God caused a deep sleep to fall on Adam, and he slept; and He took one of his ribs, and . . . made [it] into a woman, and He brought her to the man. And Adam said: "This is now bone of my bones and flesh of my flesh; she shall be called Woman, because she was taken out of Man." Therefore a man shall leave his father and mother and be joined to his wife, and they shall become one flesh.

ST. BERNADETTE
CATHOLIC CHURCH
Albuquerque, NM

ASSUMPTION CATHOLIC CHURCH
Washington, D.C.

MAN WAS DECEIVED BY SATAN AND DISOBEYED GOD

GENESIS 3:1–7A, 9, 13A, 11B, 24

Now the serpent was more cunning than any beast of the field which the LORD God had made. And he said to the woman, "Has God indeed said, 'You shall not eat of every tree of the garden'?" And the woman said to the serpent, "We may eat the fruit of the trees of the garden; but of the fruit of the tree which is in the midst of the garden, God has said, 'You shall not eat of it, nor shall you touch it, lest you die.'" Then the serpent said to the woman, "You will not surely die. For God knows that in the day you eat of it your eyes will be opened, and you will be like God, knowing good and evil." So when the woman saw that the tree was good for food, that it was pleasant to the eyes, and a tree desirable to make one wise, she took of its fruit and ate. She also gave to her husband with her, and he ate. Then the eyes of both of them were opened, and they knew that they were naked. Then the LORD God called to Adam and said to him, "Where are you? What is this you have done? Have you eaten from the tree of which I commanded you that you should not eat?" So He drove out the man; and He placed cherubim at the east of the garden of Eden, and a flaming sword which turned every way, to guard the way to the tree of life.

NOAH FOUND GRACE
IN THE EYES OF THE LORD
GENESIS VI 8

UNITED STATES NAVAL
ACADEMY CHAPEL
Annapolis, MD

Except for Noah and his family, God grieved over the wickedness of mankind

GENESIS 6:1A, 5–8, 13A, 14A, 17–19, 22

Now it came to pass men began to multiply on the face of the earth . . . The LORD saw that the wickedness of man was great in the earth, and that every intent of the thoughts of his heart was only evil continually. And the LORD was sorry that He had made man on the earth, and He was grieved in His heart. So the LORD said, "I will destroy man whom I have created from the face of the earth, both man and beast, creeping thing and birds of the air, for I am sorry that I have made them." But Noah found grace in the eyes of the LORD. And God said to Noah . . . "Make yourself an ark of gopherwood . . . and behold, I Myself am bringing floodwaters on the earth . . . everything that is on the earth shall die. But I will establish My covenant with you; and you shall go into the ark—you, your sons, your wife, and your sons' wives with you. And of every living thing of all flesh you shall bring two of every sort into the ark, to keep them alive with you; they shall be male and female." Thus Noah did; according to all that God commanded him, so he did.

FIRST BAPTIST CHURCH | *Martinsville, VA*

God caused a flood to destroy all life on earth, but made a promise

GENESIS 7:17, 23; 8:1, 15–17A; 9:11, 13

Now the flood was on the earth forty days. The waters increased and lifted up the ark, and it rose high above the earth. So He destroyed all living things which were on the face of the ground: both man and cattle, creeping thing and bird of the air. They were destroyed from the earth. Only Noah and those who were with him in the ark remained alive. Then God remembered Noah . . . and all the animals that were with him in the ark. And God made a wind to pass over the earth, and the waters subsided. Then God spoke to Noah, saying, "Go out of the ark . . . bring out with you every living thing of all flesh that is with you. Thus I establish My covenant with you . . . Never again shall there be a flood to destroy the earth. I set My rainbow in the cloud, and it shall be for the sign of the covenant between Me and the earth."

ABRAHAM, PATRIARCH OF GOD'S PEOPLE AND THE MESSIAH, AND THE FRIEND OF GOD

GENESIS 12:1–2A; 17:1–2A, 5; 21:2A, 6–7

Now the LORD had said to Abram: "Get out of your country, from your family . . . to a land that I will show you. I will make you a great nation; I will bless you and make your name great." When Abram was ninety-nine years old, the LORD appeared . . . and said to him, "I am Almighty God; walk before Me and be blameless. And I will make My covenant between Me and you . . . No longer shall your name be called Abram, but your name shall be Abraham; for I have made you a father of many nations." Sarah conceived and bore Abraham a son in his old age . . . and Sarah said, "God has made me laugh, and all who hear will laugh with me. Who would have said to Abraham that Sarah would nurse children? For I have borne him a son in his old age."

JAMES 2:23

Abraham believed God, and it was accounted to him for righteousness. And he was called the friend of God.

JOHN 8:54A, 56, 58

Jesus answered . . . "Your father Abraham rejoiced to see My day and he saw it and was glad. Most assuredly, I say to you, before Abraham was, I AM."

MOSES WAS GOD'S LAWGIVER WHO LED HIS PEOPLE OUT OF SLAVERY FROM EGYPT

EXODUS 3:4B–5, 7–8A, 10–11A, 13–14, 20

God called to him from the midst of the bush and said, "Moses, Moses!" And he said, "Here I am." Then He [God] said, "Do not draw near this place. Take your sandals off your feet, for the place where you stand is holy ground . . . I have surely seen the oppression of My people who are in Egypt, and

CHAPEL AT THE UNIVERSITY OF VIRGINIA
Charlottesville, VA

have heard their cry because of their taskmasters, for I know their sorrows. So I have come down to deliver them out of the hand of the Egyptians, and to bring them up . . . to a good and large land . . . flowing with milk and honey . . . Come now . . . and I will send you to Pharaoh that you may bring My people . . . out of Egypt." But Moses said to God, "Who am I that I should go to Pharaoh . . . indeed, when I come to the children of Israel . . . what shall I say to them?" And God said to Moses, "I AM WHO I AM." Thus you shall say . . . I AM has sent me to you. So I will stretch out My hand and strike Egypt with all My wonders which I will do in its midst; and after that he will let you go."

COLLEGE PARK
BAPTIST CHURCH
Danville, VA

THE TEN COMMANDMENTS, WHICH GOD GAVE TO MOSES ON MOUNT SINAI

EXODUS 19:3–5, 8A, 18

And Moses went up to God, and the LORD called to him from the mountain, saying, "Thus you shall . . . tell the children of Israel: 'You have seen what I did to the Egyptians, and how I bore you on eagles' wings and brought you to Myself. Now therefore, if you will indeed obey My voice and keep My covenant, then you shall be a special treasure to Me above all people . . .'" Then all the people answered together and said, "All that the LORD has spoken we will do." Now Mount Sinai was completely in smoke, because the LORD descended upon it in fire . . . and the whole mountain quaked greatly.

MATTHEW 22:36–39

"Teacher, which is the great commandment in the law?" Jesus said to him, "'You shall love the LORD your God with all your heart, with all your soul, and with all your mind.' This is the first and great commandment. And the second is like it: 'You shall love your neighbor as yourself.'"

BIBLEWAY WORLDWIDE CHURCH | *Danville, VA*

THE PEOPLE CHOSE TO WORSHIP AN IDOL INSTEAD OF THE GOD WHO FREED THEM

EXODUS 32:1A, 4, 7, 10A, 11A, 13A, 19, 30

Now when . . . Moses delayed coming down from the mountain, the people gathered together to Aaron, and said to him, "Come, make us gods that shall go before us." And he received the gold from their hand, and . . . made a molded calf. Then they said, "This is your god . . . that brought you out of the land of Egypt!" And the LORD said to Moses, "Go, get down! For your people . . . have corrupted themselves. Now . . . let Me alone, that My wrath may burn hot against them and I may consume them." Then Moses pleaded with the LORD his God . . . "Remember . . . Your servants, to whom You swore by Your own self . . ." As soon as he came near the camp, he saw the calf and the dancing. So Moses' anger became hot, and he cast the tablets out of his hands and broke them at the foot of the mountain. Moses said to the people, "You have committed a great sin. So now I will go up to the LORD; perhaps I can make atonement for your sin."

THY PEOPLE SHALL BE MY

...OPLE AND THY GOD MY GOD

A LOVE STORY OF RUTH, AN OUTCAST, WHO WAS THE GREAT-GRANDMOTHER OF DAVID

RUTH 1:1–6, 8–9, 14B,
16, 19A; 2:2A, 3; 4:13A

N ow it came to pass . . . that there was a famine in the land. And a certain man of Bethlehem, Judah, went to dwell in the country of Moab, he and his wife and his two sons. The name of his wife was Naomi. Then . . . Naomi's husband died . . . and her two sons . . . took wives of the women of Moab . . . and they . . . also died; so the woman survived her two sons and her husband. Then she arose with her daughters-in-law that she might return from the country of Moab. And Naomi said to her two daughters-in-law, "Go, return each to her mother's house . . . The LORD grant that you may find rest . . ." So she kissed them, and they lifted up their voices and wept . . . but Ruth clung to her . . . and she said: "Entreat me not to leave you, or to turn back from following after you; for wherever you go, I will go; and wherever you lodge, I will lodge; your people shall be my people, and your God, my God." Now the two of them went until they came to Bethlehem. So Ruth . . . went and gleaned in the field after the reapers . . . the part of the field belonging to Boaz. So Boaz took Ruth and she became his wife.

ST. ANDREW'S EPISCOPAL CHURCH
Richmond, VA

DAVID WAS THE GREAT KING OF ISRAEL, A SWEET PSALMIST, AND A MAN AFTER GOD'S OWN HEART

1 SAMUEL 16:1, 13; 17:20, 26, 50
Now the LORD said to Samuel . . . "Fill your horn with oil, and go; I am sending you to Jesse the Bethlehemite. For I have provided Myself a king among his sons." Then Samuel . . . anointed [David] in the midst of his brothers; and the Spirit of the LORD came upon David from that day forward. David rose early in the morning, left the sheep with a keeper . . . and came to the camp as the army was going out to fight . . . Then David spoke . . . "Who is this uncircumcised Philistine, that he should defy the armies of the living God?" So David prevailed over the Philistine with a sling and a stone, and struck the Philistine and killed him.

2 SAMUEL 8:15, 5:4B; 23:1; 22:33, 40
So David reigned over all Israel; and David administered judgment and justice to all his people. And he reigned forty years. "Thus says David the son of Jesse . . . the anointed of the God of Jacob, and the sweet psalmist of Israel: God is my strength and power, and He makes my way perfect. For You have armed me with strength for the battle; You have subdued under me those who rose against me."

ACTS 13:22B
[So God said], "I have found David the son of Jesse, a man after My own heart, who will do all My will."

JONAH DISOBEYED GOD'S ORDERS AND ENDED UP IN THE BELLY OF A WHALE

JONAH 1:1–6, 12,15,17;
2:1A, 10; 3:3A, 4B, 10B

Now the word of the LORD came to Jonah . . . saying, "Arise, go to Nineveh, that great city, and cry out against it; for their wickedness has come up before Me." But Jonah arose to flee . . . from the presence of the LORD . . . and found a ship going to Tarshish . . . But the LORD sent a . . . mighty tempest on the sea . . . and every man cried out to his god . . . but Jonah . . . was fast asleep. So the captain came to him, and said . . . "Arise, call on your God . . . so that we may not perish." And he said . . . "Pick me up and throw me into the sea . . . for I know that this great tempest is because of me." So they picked up Jonah and threw him into the sea, and the sea ceased from its raging. Now the LORD had prepared a great fish to swallow Jonah. And Jonah was in the belly of the fish three days and three nights. Then Jonah prayed to the LORD . . . so the LORD spoke to the fish, and it vomited Jonah onto dry land. So Jonah arose and went to Nineveh . . . cried out and said, "Yet forty days, and Nineveh shall be overthrown!" They turned from their evil way; and God relented.

BIBLEWAY WORLDWIDE CHURCH | *Danville, VA*

ELIJAH, A FIERY PROPHET OF THE LORD

1 KINGS 18:17–18, 21, 24A, 38A, 39–40; 2 KINGS 2:1, 11B

When [King] Ahab saw Elijah, Ahab said to him, "Is that you, O troubler of Israel?" And he answered, "I have not troubled Israel, but you and your father's house have, in that you have forsaken the commandments of the LORD and followed the Baals." And Elijah came to all the people, and said, "How long will you falter between two opinions? If the LORD is God, follow Him; but if Baal, follow him. Call on the name of your gods, and I will call on the name of the LORD; and the God who answers by fire, He is God." Then the fire of the LORD fell and consumed the burnt sacrifice, and . . . when all the people saw it, they fell on their faces; and they said, "The LORD, He is God! The LORD, He is God!" And Elijah said to them, "Seize the prophets of Baal! Do not let one of them escape!" So they seized them; and Elijah . . . executed them there. And it came to pass, when the LORD was about to take up Elijah into heaven by a whirlwind . . . that suddenly a chariot of fire appeared with horses of fire . . . and Elijah went up by a whirlwind into heaven.

"Come now, let us reason together," says the Lord, "though your sins are like scarlet, they shall be white as snow. Alas, sinful nation, a people laden with iniquity, a brood of evildoers, children who are corrupters! They have forsaken the Lord, they have provoked to anger the Holy One."

The Gift

JESUS, THE GIFT OF GOD TO MAKE RESTITUTION FOR US BY HIS SACRIFICE

JOHN 3:16;
7:42; 1:14;
1 PETER 1:15,
18–19

TIKVAT ISRAEL
CONGREGATION
Richmond, VA

FROM THE LAW TO THE MESSIAH, WE, AS CHILDREN OF GOD, HAVE JEWISH ROOTS

ISAIAH 11:1–2

There shall come forth a Rod from the stem of Jesse, and a Branch shall grow out of his roots. The Spirit of the LORD shall rest upon Him, the Spirit of wisdom and understanding, the Spirit of counsel and might, the Spirit of knowledge and of the fear of the Lord.

REVELATION 22:16

"I, Jesus, have sent My angel to testify to you these things in the churches. I am the Root and the Offspring of David, the Bright and Morning Star."

JEREMIAH 31:31, 33B

"Behold, the days are coming," says the LORD, "when I will make a new covenant with the house of Israel . . . I will put My law in their minds, and write it on their hearts; and I will be their God, and they shall be My people."

[J esus said:] "For God so loved the world that He gave His only begotten Son, that whoever believes in Him should not perish but have everlasting life. Has not the Scripture said that the Christ comes from the seed of David and from the town of Bethlehem, where David was?" And the Word became flesh and dwelt among us, and we beheld His glory, the glory as of the only begotten of the Father, full of grace and truth. He who called you is holy, you also be holy . . . knowing that you were not redeemed with corruptible things, like silver or gold . . . but with the precious blood of Christ, as of a lamb without blemish and without spot.

ST. JOSEPH'S
CATHOLIC
CHURCH
Petersburg, VA

Madeleine Demaison
Pouget

MARY, A VIRGIN, IS CHOSEN BY GOD TO BEAR HIS SON

LUKE 1:46–50, 54–55; MATTHEW 1:22–23

GABRIEL ANNOUNCES TO MARY THAT SHE WILL BE MOTHER TO THE SON OF GOD

LUKE 1:26–32, 34–35

Now . . . the angel Gabriel was sent by God to a city of Galilee named Nazareth, to a virgin betrothed to a man who was named Joseph, of the house of David. The virgin's name was Mary. And having come in, the angel said to her, "Rejoice, highly favored one, the Lord is with you; blessed are you among women!" But when she saw him, she was troubled at his saying, and considered what manner of greeting this was. Then the angel said to her, "Do not be afraid, Mary, for you have found favor with God. And behold, you will conceive in your womb and bring forth a Son, and shall call His name JESUS. He will be great, and will be called the Son of the Highest; and the LORD God will give him the throne of His

Behold the handmaid of the LORD

CHRIST EPISCOPAL CHURCH | *Roanoke, VA*

And Mary said: "My soul magnifies the LORD, and my spirit has rejoiced in God my Savior. For He has regarded the lowly state of His maidservant; for behold, henceforth all generations will call me blessed. For He who is mighty has done great things for me, and holy is His name. And His mercy is on those who fear Him from generation to generation. He has helped His servant Israel, in remembrance of His mercy, as He spoke to our fathers, to Abraham and to his seed forever."

This was done that it might be fulfilled which was spoken by the LORD through the prophet, saying: "Behold, the virgin shall be with child, and bear a Son, and they shall call His name Immanuel," which is translated, "God with us."

father, David." Then Mary said to the angel, "How can this be, since I do not know a man?" And the angel answered and said to her, "The Holy Spirit will come upon you, and the power of the Highest will overshadow you; therefore, also, that Holy One who is to be born will be called the Son of God."

TRINITY
EPISCOPAL
CHURCH
Rocky Mount, VA

MARY VISITS ELIZABETH, WHO WILL BE THE MOTHER OF JOHN THE BAPTIST

LUKE 1:36–43

[The angel Gabriel said:] "Now indeed, Elizabeth your relative has also conceived a son in her old age; and this is now the sixth month for her who was called barren. For with God nothing will be impossible." Then Mary said, "Behold the maidservant of the Lord! Let it be to me according to your word." And the angel departed from her. Now Mary arose in those days and went into the hill country with haste, to a city of Judah, and entered the house of Zacharias and greeted Elizabeth. And it happened, when Elizabeth heard the greeting of Mary, that the babe leaped in her womb; and Elizabeth was filled with the Holy Spirit. Then she spoke out with a loud voice and said, "Blessed are you among women, and blessed is the fruit of your womb! But why is this granted to me, that the mother of my Lord should come to me?"

THE BIRTH OF JESUS

LUKE 2:1, 3–7

And it came to pass in those days that a decree went out from Caesar Augustus that all the world should be registered. So all went to be registered, everyone to his own city. Joseph also went up from Galilee, out of the city of Nazareth, into Judea, to the city of David, which is called Bethlehem, because he was of the house and lineage of David, to be registered with Mary, his betrothed wife, who was with child. So it was, that while they were there, the days were completed for her to be delivered. And she brought forth her firstborn Son, and wrapped Him in swaddling cloths, and laid Him in a manger, because there was no room for them in the inn.

TRINITY EPISCOPAL CHURCH *Staunton, VA*

BETHANY
UNITED
METHODIST
CHURCH
Reedville, VA

JESUS IS BORN! BEHOLD, THE NATIVITY

LUKE 2:16–20

AN ANGEL ANNOUNCES THE BIRTH OF JESUS TO SHEPHERDS IN THE FIELDS

LUKE 2:8–15

Now there were in the same country shepherds living out in the fields, keeping watch over their flock by night. And behold, an angel of the Lord stood before them . . . and they were greatly afraid. Then the angel said to them, "Do not be afraid, for behold, I bring you good tidings of great joy which will be to all people. For there is born to you this day in the city of David a Savior, who is Christ the Lord. And this will be the sign to you: You will find a Babe wrapped in swaddling cloths, lying in a manger." And suddenly there was with the angel a multitude of the heavenly host praising God and saying, "Glory to God in the highest, and on earth peace, goodwill toward men!" So it was, when the angels had gone away from them into heaven, that the shepherds said to one another, "Let us now go to Bethlehem and see this thing that has come to pass, which the Lord has made known to us."

And they came with haste and found Mary and Joseph, and the Babe lying in a manger. Now when they had seen Him, they made widely known the saying which was told them concerning this Child. And all those who heard it marveled at those things which were told them by the shepherds. But Mary kept all these things and pondered them in her heart. Then the shepherds returned, glorifying and praising God for all the things that they had heard and seen, as it was told them.

TRINITY EPISCOPAL CHURCH
Wilmington, DE

JESUS IS PRESENTED TO THE PRIESTS IN THE TEMPLE

LUKE 2:21–24

THE JOYS OF A FIRST-BORN SON

MATTHEW 1:21

"And she will bring forth a Son, and you shall call his name JESUS, for He will save His people from their sins."

LUKE 2:33

And Joseph and His mother marveled at those things which were spoken of Him.

JOHN 1:1, 4, 9

In the beginning was the Word, and the Word was with God, and the Word was God. In Him was life, and the life was the light of men. That was the true Light which gives light to every man coming into the world.

THE LIGHT OF THE WORLD

And when eight days were completed for the circumcision of the Child, His name was called JESUS, the name given by the angel before He was conceived in the womb. Now when the days of her purification according to the law of Moses were completed, they brought Him to Jerusalem to present Him to the Lord (as it is written in the law of the Lord, "Every male who opens the womb shall be called holy to the LORD"), and to offer a sacrifice according to what is said in the law of the Lord, "A pair of turtledoves or two young pigeons."

MEADE MEMORIAL EPISCOPAL CHURCH *Alexandria, VA*

WISE MEN FOLLOW A STAR TO SEE A KING

MATTHEW 2:1–4, 7–10

Now after Jesus was born in Bethlehem of Judea in the days of Herod the king, behold, wise men from the East came to Jerusalem, saying, "Where is He who has been born King of the Jews? For we have seen His star in the East and have come to worship Him." When Herod the king heard this, he was troubled, and all Jerusalem with him. And when he had gathered all the chief priests and scribes of the people together, he inquired of them where the Christ was to be born. Then Herod, when he had secretly called the wise men, determined from them what time the star appeared. And he sent them to Bethlehem and said, "Go and search carefully for the young Child, and when you have found Him, bring back word to me, that I may come and worship Him also." When they heard the king, they departed; and behold, the star which they had seen in the East went before them, till it came and stood over where the young Child was. When they saw the star, they rejoiced with exceedingly great joy.

THEY FIND HIM AND PRESENT THE CHILD WITH FINE GIFTS

MATTHEW 2:11–12

And when they had come into the house, they saw the young Child with Mary, His mother, and fell down and worshiped Him. And when they had opened their treasures, they presented gifts to Him: gold, frankincense, and myrrh. Then, being divinely warned in a dream that they should not return to Herod, they departed for their own country another way.

FIRST ENGLISH LUTHERAN CHURCH
Baltimore, MD

REJOICED WITH EXCEEDING GREAT JOY

GOD WARNS JOSEPH TO LEAVE THE COUNTRY WITH HIS WIFE AND CHILD

MATTHEW 2:13–16, 19–20

A MOTHER AND CHILD SEE SORROW IN THEIR FUTURE

ISAIAH 9:6

For unto us a Child is born, unto us a Son is given; and the government will be upon His shoulder. And His name will be called Wonderful, Counselor, Mighty God, Everlasting Father, Prince of Peace.

LUKE 2:25A, 26–32, 34–35A

And behold, there was a man . . . whose name was Simeon, and this man was just and devout . . . and it had been revealed to him by the Holy Spirit that he would not see death before he had seen the Lord's Christ . . . And when the parents brought in the Child Jesus . . . he took Him up in his arms and blessed God and said, "Lord, now you are letting Your servant depart in peace, according to Your word; for my eyes have seen Your salvation which You have prepared before the face of all peoples, a light to bring revelation to the Gentiles, and the glory of Your people Israel." Then Simeon blessed them, and said to Mary His mother, "Behold, this Child is destined for the fall and rising of many in Israel, and . . . (yes, a sword will pierce through your own soul also).

ST. JOHN'S EPISCOPAL CHURCH | *Tappahannock, VA*

Now when they had departed, behold, an angel of the Lord appeared to Joseph in a dream, saying, "Arise, take the young Child and His mother, flee to Egypt, and stay there until I bring you word; for Herod will seek the young Child to destroy Him." When he arose, he took the young Child and His mother by night and departed for Egypt, and was there until the death of Herod, that it might be fulfilled which was spoken by the Lord through the prophet, saying, "Out of Egypt I called My Son." Then Herod, when he saw that he was deceived by the wise men, was exceedingly angry; and he sent forth and put to death all the male children who were in Bethlehem and in all its districts, from two years old and under, according to the time which he had determined from the wise men. Now when Herod was dead, behold, an angel of the Lord appeared in a dream to Joseph in Egypt, saying, "Arise, take the young Child and His mother, and go to the land of Israel, for those who sought the young Child's life are dead."

TRINITY
EPISCOPAL
CHURCH
Rocky Mount, VA

AS JESUS DIALOGUES IN THE TEMPLE, HIS MOTHER WONDERS WHERE HE IS

LUKE 2:41–50

SS. PETER & PAUL CATHOLIC CHURCH
Cumberland, MD

OLD SWEDES CHURCH, TRINITY PARISH
Wilmington, DE

His parents went to Jerusalem every year at the Feast of the Passover. And when He was twelve years old, they went up to Jerusalem according to the custom of the feast. When they had finished the days, as they returned, the Boy Jesus lingered behind in Jerusalem. And Joseph and His mother did not know it; but supposing Him to have been in the company, they went a day's journey, and sought Him among their relatives and acquaintances. So when they did not find Him, they returned to Jerusalem, seeking Him. Now so it was that after three days they found Him in the temple, sitting in the midst of the teachers, both listening to them and asking them questions. And all who heard Him were astonished at His understanding and answers. So when they saw Him, they were amazed; and His mother said to Him, "Son, why have You done this to us? Look, Your father and I have sought You anxiously." And He said to them, "Why did you seek Me? Did you not know that I must be about My Father's business?" But they did not understand the statement which He spoke to them.

THE HOLY FAMILY IN NAZARETH

LUKE 2:51, 40, 52

Then He went down with them and came to Nazareth, and was subject to them, but His mother kept all these things in her heart. And the Child grew and became strong in spirit, filled with wisdom; and the grace of God was upon Him. Jesus increased in wisdom and stature, and in favor with God and men.

SAINT AUGUSTINE
CHURCH [CATHOLIC]
Washington, D.C.

PSALM 119:105

Your word is a lamp to my
feet and a light to my path.

JOHN 1:14

And the Word became
flesh and dwelt among us,
and we beheld His glory,
the glory as of the only
begotten of the Father, full
of grace and truth.

ST. ANDREW'S
EPISCOPAL
CHURCH
Burke, VA

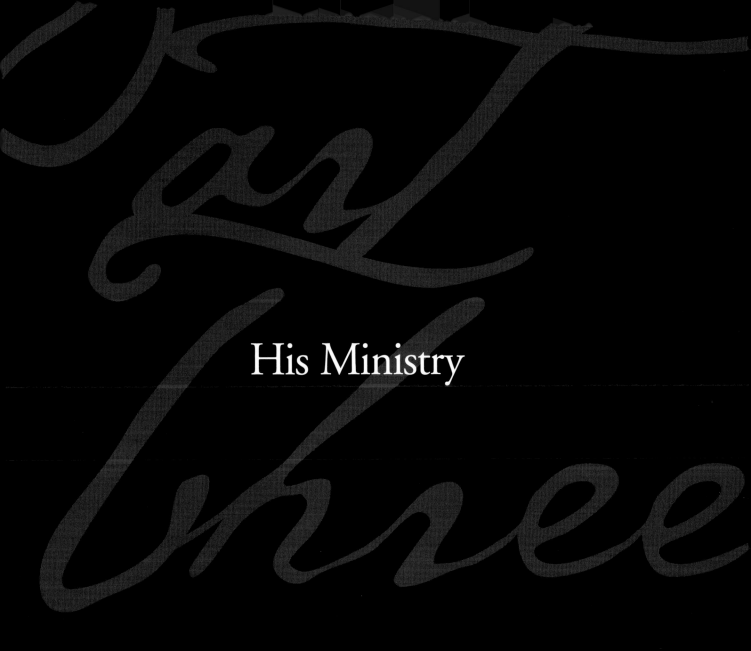

His Ministry

THE EPISCOPAL
CHURCH
OF THE EPIPHANY
Danville, VA

JOHN, JESUS' COUSIN, PREPARES THE PEOPLE FOR THE MESSIAH AND GOD'S KINGDOM

MATTHEW 3:1–6, 11

I n those days John the Baptist came preaching in the wilderness of Judea, and saying, "Repent, for the kingdom of heaven is at hand!" For this is he who was spoken of by the prophet Isaiah, saying, "The voice of one crying in the wilderness: 'Prepare the way of the LORD; make His paths straight.'" Now John himself was clothed in camel's hair, with a leather belt around his waist; and his food was locusts and wild honey. Then Jerusalem, all Judea, and all the region around the Jordan went out to him and were baptized by him in the Jordan, confessing their sins, [as John said,] "I indeed baptize you with water unto repentance, but He who is coming after me is mightier than I, whose sandals I am not worthy to carry. He will baptize you with the Holy Spirit and fire."

ST. KATHERINE'S
GREEK
ORTHODOX
CHURCH
Falls Church, VA

BIBLEWAY WORLDWIDE CHURCH | *Danville, VA*

JESUS IS BAPTIZED, IDENTIFYING HIM AS THE MESSIAH AND IS AFFIRMED BY HIS FATHER, GOD

MATTHEW 3:13–17

Then Jesus came from Galilee to John at the Jordan to be baptized by him. And John tried to prevent Him, saying, "I need to be baptized by You, and You are coming to me?" But Jesus answered and said to him, "Permit it to be so now, for thus it is fitting for us to fulfill all righteousness." Then he allowed Him. When He had been baptized, Jesus came up immediately from the water; and behold, the heavens were opened to Him, and He saw the Spirit of God descending like a dove and alighting upon Him. And suddenly a voice came from heaven, saying, "This is My beloved Son, in whom I am well pleased."

TRINITY
EPISCOPAL
CHURCH
Fredericksburg, VA

JESUS IS TEMPTED BY SATAN AND USES THE WORD OF GOD TO DRIVE HIM AWAY

MATTHEW 4:1–4, 8–11

Then Jesus was led up by the Spirit into the wilderness to be tempted by the devil. And when He had fasted forty days and forty nights, afterward He was hungry. Now when the tempter came to Him, he said, "If You are the Son of God, command that these stones become bread." But He answered and said, "It is written, 'Man shall not live by bread alone, but by every word that proceeds from the mouth of God.'" Again, the devil took him up on an exceedingly high mountain, and showed Him all the kingdoms of the world and their glory. And he said to Him, "All these things I will give You if You will fall down and worship me." Then Jesus said to him, "Away with you, Satan! For it is written, 'You shall worship the LORD your God, and Him only you shall serve.'" Then the devil left Him, and behold, angels came and ministered to Him.

ST. JOHN'S UNITED CHURCH OF CHRIST
Richmond, VA

JESUS ANNOUNCES HIS MINISTRY

LUKE 4:16–21

So He came to Nazareth, where He had been brought up. And as His custom was, He went into the synagogue on the Sabbath day, and stood up to read. And He was handed the book of the prophet Isaiah. And when He had opened the book, He found the place where it was written: "The Spirit of the LORD is upon me, because He has anointed Me to preach the gospel to the poor; He has sent Me to heal the brokenhearted, to proclaim liberty to the captives and recovery of sight to the blind, to set at liberty those who are oppressed; to proclaim the acceptable year of the LORD." Then He closed the book, and gave it back to the attendant and sat down. And the eyes of all who were in the synagogue were fixed on Him. And He began to say to them, "Today this Scripture is fulfilled in your hearing."

JESUS CALLS FOUR FISHERMEN TO BE HIS DISCIPLES

MATTHEW 4:17–22

From that time Jesus began to preach and to say, "Repent, for the kingdom of heaven is at hand." And Jesus, walking by the Sea of Galilee, saw two brothers, Simon called Peter, and Andrew his brother, casting a net into the sea; for they were fishermen. Then He said to them, "Follow Me, and I will make you fishers of men." They immediately left their nets and followed Him. Going on from there, He saw two other brothers, James the son of Zebedee, and John his brother, in the boat with Zebedee their father, mending their nets. He called them, and immediately they left the boat and their father, and followed Him.

GRACE EPISCOPAL CHURCH
Berryville, VA

THEN HE CALLS A SHUNNED TAX COLLECTOR

MATTHEW 9:9–13

As Jesus passed on from there, He saw a man named Matthew sitting at the tax office. And He said to him, "Follow Me." So he arose and followed Him. Now it happened, as Jesus sat at the table in the house, that behold, many tax collectors and sinners came and sat down with Him and His disciples. And when the Pharisees saw it, they said to His disciples, "Why does your Teacher eat with tax collectors and sinners?" When Jesus heard that, He said to them, "Those who are well have no need of a physician, but those who are sick. But go and learn what this means: 'I desire mercy and not sacrifice.' For I did not come to call the righteous, but sinners, to repentance."

ST. JOHN'S
EPISCOPAL CHURCH
Hagerstown, MD

JESUS MAKES 150 GALLONS OF WINE AT A FESTIVE WEDDING IN CANA

JOHN 2:1–11

There was a wedding in Cana of Galilee, and the mother of Jesus was there. Now both Jesus and His disciples were invited to the wedding. And when they ran out of wine, the mother of Jesus said to Him, "They have no wine." Jesus said to her, "Woman, what does your concern have to do with Me? My hour has not yet come." His mother said to the servants, "Whatever He says to you, do it." Now there were . . . six waterpots of stone . . . containing twenty or thirty gallons apiece. Jesus said to them, "Fill the waterpots with water." They filled them . . . and He said to them, "Draw some out now, and take it to the master of the feast." When the master of the feast had tasted the water that was made wine, and did not know where it came from . . . he called the bridegroom. And he said to him, "Every man at the beginning sets out the good wine, and when the guests have well drunk, then the inferior. You have kept the good wine until now!" This beginning of signs Jesus did in Cana of Galilee, and manifested His glory; and His disciples believed in Him.

JESUS SATISFIES THE HUNGER OF 5,000 PEOPLE

JOHN 6:4–5, 8–13A

Now the Passover, a feast of the Jews, was near. Then Jesus lifted up His eyes, and seeing a great multitude coming toward Him, He said to Philip, "Where shall we buy bread, that these may eat?" One of His disciples, Andrew, Simon Peter's brother, said to Him, "There is a lad here who has five barley loaves and two small fish, but what are they among so many?" Then Jesus said, "Make the people sit down." Now there was much grass in the place. So the men sat down, in number about five thousand. And Jesus took the loaves, and when He had given thanks He distributed them to the disciples, and the disciples to those sitting down; and likewise of the fish, as much as they wanted. So when they were filled, He said to His disciples, "Gather up the fragments that remain, so that nothing is lost." Therefore they gathered them up, and filled twelve baskets . . .

ST. JOHN'S EPISCOPAL CHURCH | *Hagerstown, MD*

JESUS TEACHES RIGHT ATTITUDES IN THE BEATITUDES

MATTHEW 5:1–12A

And seeing the multitudes, He went up on a mountain, and when He was seated His disciples came to Him. Then He opened His mouth and taught them, saying, "Blessed are the poor in spirit, for theirs is the kingdom of heaven. Blessed are those who mourn, for they shall be comforted. Blessed are the meek, for they shall inherit the earth. Blessed are those who hunger and thirst for righteousness, for they shall be filled. Blessed are the merciful, for they shall obtain mercy. Blessed are the pure in heart, for they shall see God. Blessed are the peacemakers, for they shall be called sons of God. Blessed are those who are persecuted for righteousness' sake for theirs is the kingdom of heaven. Blessed are you when they revile and persecute you, and say all kinds of evil against you falsely for My sake. Rejoice and be exceedingly glad, for great is your reward in heaven . . ."

ST. JOHN'S UNITED CHURCH OF CHRIST | *Richmond, VA*

IN THE STORY OF THE LOST SHEEP, JESUS TELLS HOW HE FEELS ABOUT EACH ONE OF US

LUKE 15:3–7

So He spoke this parable to them, saying: "What man of you, having a hundred sheep, if he loses one of them, does not leave the ninety-nine in the wilderness, and go after the one which is lost until he finds it? And when he has found it, he lays it on his shoulders, rejoicing. And when he comes home, he calls together his friends and neighbors, saying to them, 'Rejoice with me, for I have found my sheep which was lost!' I say to you that likewise there will be more joy in heaven over one sinner who repents than over ninety-nine just persons who need no repentance."

The parable of the sower gives examples of how we receive God's Word

MARK 4:2–4, 7–8A, 14–15, 18–20

He taught them . . . by parables, and said . . . "Listen! Behold, a sower went out to sow. And it happened, as he sowed, that some seed fell by the wayside; and the birds of the air came and devoured it. And some seed fell among thorns; and the thorns grew up and choked it, and it yielded no crop. But other seed fell on good ground and yielded a crop that sprang up, increased and produced . . . The sower sows the word. And these are the ones by the wayside where the word is sown. When they hear, Satan comes immediately and takes away the word that was sown in their hearts. The ones sown among thorns; they are the ones who hear the word, and the cares of this world, the deceitfulness of riches, and the desires for other things entering in choke the word . . . But . . . the ones sown on good ground, those who hear the word, accept it, and bear fruit: some thirtyfold . . . some a hundred."

ST. JOHN'S EPISCOPAL CHURCH | *Bedford, VA*

Jesus counsels the rich young ruler whose worldly possessions come first

MATTHEW 19:16–17, 20–23

Now behold, one came and said to Him, "Good Teacher, what good thing shall I do that I may have eternal life?" So He said to him, "Why do you call Me good? No one is good but One, that is, God. But if you want to enter into life, keep the commandments." The young man said to Him, "All these things I have kept from my youth. What do I still lack?" Jesus said to him, "If you want to be perfect, go, sell what you have and give to the poor, and you will have treasure in heaven; and come, follow Me." But when the young man heard that saying, he went away sorrowful, for he had great possessions. Then Jesus said to His disciples, "Assuredly, I say to you that it is hard for a rich man to enter the kingdom of heaven."

SAINT
DAVID'S
PARISH
[EPISCOPAL]

THE PEARL OF GREAT PRICE: FOR US, THE KINGDOM OF GOD; FOR JESUS—YOU!

MATTHEW 13:45–46

[J esus said,] "Again, the kingdom of heaven is like a merchant seeking beautiful pearls, who, when he had found one pearl of great price, went out and sold all that he had and bought it."

THE PRODIGAL SON: A LIFE WASTED, YET THE FATHER RUNS TO WELCOME THE REPENTANT

LUKE 15:11–13, 16, 20–24

Then He said, "A certain man had two sons. And the younger of them said to his father, 'Father, give me the portion of goods that falls to me.' So he divided to them his livelihood . . . The younger son gathered all together, journeyed to a far country, and there wasted his possessions with wasteful living and . . . began to be in want. And he would gladly have filled his stomach with the pods that the swine ate, and no one gave him anything. And he arose and came to his father. But when he was still a great way off, his father saw him and had compassion, and ran and fell on his neck and kissed him. And the son said to him, 'Father, I have sinned against heaven and in your sight, and am no longer worthy to be called your son.' But the father said to his servants, 'Bring out the best robe and put it on him . . . and bring the fatted calf here and kill it, and let us eat and be merry; for this my son was dead and is alive again; he was lost and is found.' And they began to be merry."

ST. JOHN'S UNITED CHURCH OF CHRIST
Richmond, VA

MAIN STREET
UNITED METHODIST
CHURCH
Bedford, VA

THE STORY OF THE GOOD SAMARITAN TELLS US HOW WE SHOULD LOVE OTHERS

LUKE 10:25–27, 29–37

A certain lawyer stood up and tested Him, saying, "Teacher, what shall I do to inherit eternal life?" [Jesus] said to him, "What is written in the law?" So he answered and said, "'You shall love the LORD your God with all your heart, with all your soul, with all your strength, and with all your mind,' and 'your neighbor as yourself.'" But he, wanting to justify himself, said to Jesus, "And who is my neighbor?" Then Jesus answered and said: "A certain man went down from Jerusalem to Jericho, and fell among thieves, who stripped him of his clothing, wounded him, and departed, leaving him half dead. Now by chance a certain priest came down that road. And when he saw him, he passed by on the other side. Likewise a Levite, when he arrived at the place, came and looked, and passed by on the other side. But a certain Samaritan, as he journeyed, came where he was. And when he saw him, he had compassion. So he went to him and bandaged his wounds, pouring on oil and wine; and he set him on his own animal, brought him to an inn, and took care of him. On the next day, when he departed, he took out two denarii, gave them to the innkeeper, and said to him, 'Take care of him; and whatever more you spend, when I come again, I will repay you.' So which of these three do you think was neighbor to him who fell among the thieves?" And he said, "He who showed mercy on him." Then Jesus said to him, "Go and do likewise."

MAIN STREET UNITED METHODIST CHURCH
Bedford, VA

JESUS SPEAKS TO THE WOMAN AT THE WELL

JOHN 4:7, 9–10, 13B–19, 25–26

A woman of Samaria came to draw water. Jesus said to her, "Give Me a drink." Then the woman of Samaria said to Him, "How is it that You, being a Jew, ask a drink from me, a Samaritan woman?" For Jews have no dealings with Samaritans. Jesus answered and said to her, "If you knew the gift of God, and who it is who says to you, 'Give Me a drink,' you would have asked Him, and He would have given you living water. Whoever drinks of this water will thirst again, but whoever drinks of the water that I shall give him will never thirst. But the water that I shall give him will become in him a fountain of water springing up into everlasting life." The woman said to Him, "Sir, give me this water, that I may not thirst, nor come here to draw." Jesus said to her, "Go, call your husband, and come here." The woman answered and said, "I have no husband." Jesus said to her, "You have well said, 'I have no husband,' for you have had five husbands, and the one whom you now have is not your husband; in that you spoke truly." The woman said to Him, "Sir, I perceive that you are a prophet . . . I know that Messiah is coming. When He comes, He will tell us all things." Jesus said to her, "I who speak to you am He."

EMMANUEL
EPISCOPAL
CHURCH
Rapidan, VA

If we believe in and trust our loving Father God, we do not need to worry

LUKE 12:22–23, 27–31

Then He said to His disciples, "Therefore I say to you, do not worry about your life, what you will eat; nor about the body, what you will put on. Life is more than food, and the body is more than clothing. Consider the lilies, how they grow: they neither toil nor spin; and yet I say to you, even Solomon in all his glory was not arrayed like one of these. If then God so clothes the grass, which today is in the field and tomorrow is thrown into the oven, how much more will He clothe you, O you of little faith? And do not seek what you should eat or what you should drink, nor have an anxious mind. For all these things the nations of the world seek after, and your Father knows that you need these things. But seek the kingdom of God, and all these things shall be added to you."

The difference between service and worship is illustrated

LUKE 10:38–42

Now it happened as they went that He entered a certain village; and a certain woman named Martha welcomed Him into her house. And she had a sister called Mary, who also sat at Jesus' feet and heard His word. But Martha was distracted with much serving, and she approached Him and said, "Lord, do You not care that my sister has left me to serve alone? Therefore tell her to help me." And Jesus answered and said to her, "Martha, Martha, you are worried and troubled about many things. But one thing is needed, and Mary has chosen that good part, which will not be taken away from her."

FIRST ENGLISH LUTHERAN CHURCH | *Baltimore, MD*

JESUS BLESSES A POOR WIDOW WHO GIVES FROM HER NEED

LUKE 21:1–4

And He looked up and saw the rich putting their gifts into the treasury, and He saw also a certain poor widow putting in two mites. So He said, "Truly I say to you that this poor widow has put in more than all; for all these out of their abundance have put in offerings for God, but she out of her poverty put in all the livelihood that she had."

ST. JOHN'S
UNITED CHURCH
OF CHRIST
Richmond, VA

JESUS ANSWERS BLIND BARTIMAEUS' CRIES AND HEALS HIM

MARK 10:46–52

Now they came to Jericho. As He went out of Jericho with His disciples and a great multitude, blind Bartimaeus, the son of Timaeus, sat by the road begging. And when he heard that it was Jesus of Nazareth, he began to cry out and say, "Jesus, Son of David, have mercy on me!" Then many warned him to be quiet; but he cried out all the more, "Son of David, have mercy on me!" So Jesus stood still and commanded him to be called. Then they called the blind man, saying to him, "Be of good cheer. Rise, He is calling you." And throwing aside his garment, he rose and came to Jesus. So Jesus answered and said to him, "What do you want me to do for you?" The blind man said to Him, "Rabboni, that I may receive my sight." Then Jesus said to him, "Go your way; your faith has made you well." And immediately he received his sight and followed Jesus on the road.

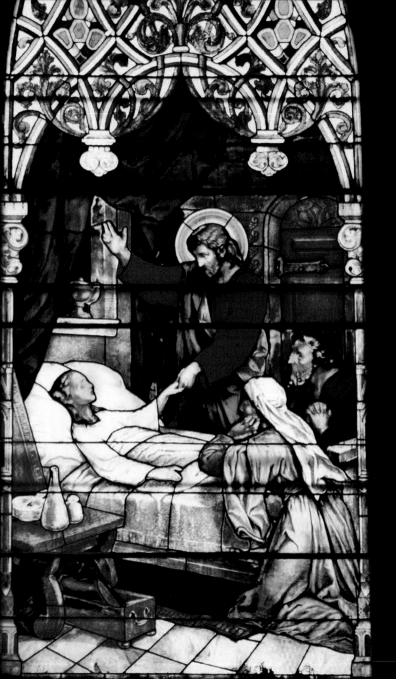

JESUS RESTORES THE DAUGHTER OF JAIRUS, A JEWISH RULER, TO LIFE

LUKE 8:41–42, 49–56

There came a man named Jairus, and he was a ruler of the synagogue. And he fell down at Jesus' feet and begged Him to come to his house, for he had an only daughter about twelve years of age, and she was dying. Someone came from the ruler of the synagogue's house, saying to him, "Your daughter is dead. Do not trouble the Teacher." But when Jesus heard it, He answered him, saying, "Do not be afraid; only believe, and she will be made well." When He came into the house, He permitted no one to go in except Peter, James, and John, and the father and mother of the girl. Now all wept and mourned for her; but He said, "Do not weep; she is not dead, but sleeping." And they ridiculed Him, knowing that she was dead. But He put them all outside, took her by the hand and called, saying, "Little girl, arise." Then her spirit returned, and she arose immediately. And He commanded that she be given something to eat. And her parents were astonished, but He charged them to tell no one what had happened.

LATER JESUS RAISES HIS FRIEND, LAZARUS, FROM THE DEAD

JOHN 11:1, 3, 17, 21–23, 25, 34–35, 38–44

Now a certain man was sick, Lazarus of Bethany, the town of Mary and her sister Martha. Therefore the sisters sent to Him, saying, "Lord, behold, he whom You love is sick." So when Jesus came, He found that he had already been in the tomb four days. Now Martha said to Jesus, "Lord, if You had been here, my brother would not have died. But even now I know that whatever You ask of God, God will give You." Jesus said to her, "Your brother will rise again. I am the resurrection and the life. He who believes in me, though he may die, he shall live." And He said, "Where have you laid him?" They said to Him, "Lord, come and see." Jesus wept. Then Jesus, again groaning in Himself, came to the tomb. Jesus said, "Take away the stone." Martha . . . said to Him, "Lord, by this time there is a stench, for he has been dead four days." Jesus said to her, "Did I not say to you that if you would believe you would see the glory of God?" Then they took away the stone . . . and Jesus lifted up His eyes and said, "Father, I thank You that You have heard me . . . that they may believe that You sent Me." When He had said these things, He cried with a loud voice, "Lazarus, come forth!" And he who had died came out bound hand and foot with graveclothes . . . Jesus said to them, "Loose him, and let him go."

TRINITY LUTHERAN CHURCH *Hagerstown, MD*

JESUS COMFORTS US

JOHN 7:37B

Jesus stood and cried out, saying, "If anyone thirsts, let him come to Me and drink."

ISAIAH 66:12–13A

For thus says the LORD: "Behold, I will extend peace to her like a river, and the glory of the Gentiles like a flowing stream. Then you shall feed; on her sides shall you be carried and be dandled on her knees. As one whom his mother comforts, so I will comfort you."

2 CORINTHIANS 1:3–5

Blessed be the God and Father of our Lord Jesus Christ, the Father of mercies and God of all comfort, who comforts us in all our tribulation, that we may be able to comfort those who are in any trouble, with the comfort with which we ourselves are comforted by God. For as the sufferings of Christ abound in us, so our consolation also abounds through Christ.

TRINITY EPISCOPAL CHURCH *Wilmington, DE*

JESUS RESCUES US FROM EVIL AND ALL THAT BINDS AND TORMENTS OUR SOULS

MARK 5:2–3, 5–9, 11–13, 15

There met Him . . . a man with an unclean spirit, who had his dwelling among the tombs; and no one could bind him, not even with chains . . . And always, night and day, he was . . . crying out and cutting himself with stones. When he saw Jesus from afar, he ran and worshiped Him. And he cried out with a loud voice and said, "What have I to do with You, Jesus, Son of the Most High God? I implore You by God that You do not torment me." For He said to him, "Come out of the man, unclean spirit!" Then He asked him, "What is your name?" And he answered, saying, "My name is Legion; for we are many." Now a large herd of swine was feeding there near the mountains. So all the demons begged Him, saying, "Send us to the swine, that we may enter them." And at once, Jesus gave them permission . . . and the herd ran violently down the steep place into the sea, and drowned . . . Then they . . . saw the one who had been demon-possessed . . . clothed and in his right mind. And they were afraid.

JESUS HEALS ALL OF US, THOUGH NOT ALWAYS IN THE WAY WE WOULD EXPECT

MATTHEW 9:35

Then Jesus went about all the cities and villages, teaching in their synagogues, preaching the gospel of the kingdom, and healing every sickness and every disease among the people.

MATTHEW 15:31

So the multitude marveled when they saw the mute speaking, the maimed made whole, the lame walking, and the blind seeing; and they glorified the God of Israel.

MATTHEW 12:14

Then the Pharisees went out and plotted against Him, how they might destroy Him.

JOHN WESLEY UNITED METHODIST CHURCH
Hagerstown, MD

SUFFER THE LITTLE CHILDREN

JESUS LOVES LITTLE CHILDREN

MARK 10:13–16

Then they brought little children to Him, that He might touch them; but the disciples rebuked those who brought them. But when Jesus saw it, He was greatly displeased and said to them, "Let the little children come to Me, and do not forbid them; for of such is the kingdom of God. Assuredly, I say to you, whoever does not receive the kingdom of God as a little child will by no means enter it." And He took them up in His arms, laid His hands on them, and blessed them.

OUR FATHER
WHICH
ART
IN
HEAVEN

ST. STEPHEN'S
EPISCOPAL CHURCH
Richmond, VA

JESUS WILL TEACH US TO PRAY TO OUR FATHER IN HEAVEN AND ASKS US TO FORGIVE OTHERS

MATTHEW 5:1–2;
6:9–15

And seeing the multitudes, He went up on a mountain, and when He was seated his disciples came to Him. Then He opened His mouth and taught them, saying, "In this manner, therefore, pray: Our Father in heaven, hallowed be Your name. Your kingdom come. Your will be done on earth as it is in heaven. Give us this day our daily bread. And forgive us our debts, as we forgive our debtors. And do not lead us into temptation, but deliver us from the evil one. For Yours is the kingdom and the power and the glory forever. Amen. For if you forgive men their trespasses, your heavenly Father will also forgive you. But if you do not forgive men their trespasses, neither will your Father forgive your trespasses."

JOHN WESLEY UNITED METHODIST CHURCH | *Hagerstown, MD*

AS OUR HIGH PRIEST, JESUS PRAYS TO THE FATHER ON OUR BEHALF

HEBREWS 7:25–27
Therefore He is also able to save to the uttermost those who come to God through Him, since He always lives to make intercession for them. For such a High Priest was fitting for us, who is holy, harmless, undefiled, separate from sinners, and has become higher than the heavens; who does not need daily, as those high priests, to offer up sacrifices, first for His own sins and then for the people's, for this He did once for all when He offered up Himself.

JOHN 17:1A, 20–21, 23B
Jesus spoke these words, lifted up His eyes up to heaven, and said: "Father. . . I . . . pray . . . for those who will believe in Me through the word; that they all may be one, as You, Father, are in Me, and I in You; that they also may be one in Us, that the world may believe that You sent Me. And the glory which You gave Me I have given them, that they may be one just as We are one . . . and have loved them as You have loved Me."

JESUS WALKS ON WATER, PETER SINKS

MATTHEW 14:22–31, 33

Jesus made His disciples get into the boat and go before Him to the other side . . . and He went up on the mountain by Himself to pray. But the boat was now in the middle of the sea, tossed by the waves, for the wind was contrary. Now in the fourth watch of the night Jesus went to them, walking on the sea. And when the disciples saw Him . . . they were troubled, saying, "It is a ghost!" And they cried out for fear. Jesus spoke to them, saying, "Be of good cheer! It is I; do not be afraid." And Peter answered Him and said, "Lord, if it is You, command me to come to You on the water." So He said, "Come." And . . . he walked on the water to go to Jesus. But when he saw that the wind was boisterous, he was afraid; and beginning to sink he cried out, saying, "Lord save me!" And immediately Jesus stretched out His hand and caught him, and said to him, "O, you of little faith, why did you doubt?" Then those who were in the boat came and worshiped Him, saying, "Truly You are the Son of God."

PETER PROCLAIMS THAT JESUS IS THE SON OF GOD, WHICH IS THE ROCK OF OUR FAITH

MATTHEW 16:13–18

When Jesus came . . . He asked His disciples, saying, "Who do men say that I, the Son of Man, am?" So they said, "Some say John the Baptist, some Elijah, and others Jeremiah or one of the prophets." He said to them, "But who do you say I am?" Simon Peter answered and said, "You are the Christ, the Son of the living God." Jesus answered and said to him, "Blessed are you, Simon Bar-Jonah, for flesh and blood has not revealed this to you, but My Father who is in heaven. And I also say to you that you are Peter, and on this rock I will build My church, and the gates of Hades shall not prevail against it."

EMMANUEL CHURCH
AT BROOK HILL [EPISCOPAL]
Richmond, VA

Thomas said to Him, "Lord, we do not know where You are going, and how can we know the way?" Jesus said to him, "I am the way, the truth, and the life. No one comes to the Father except through Me."

Then Jesus said to them again, "Most assuredly, I say to you, I am the door of the sheep. If anyone enters by Me, he will be saved, and will go in and out and find pasture. I am the good shepherd. The good shepherd gives His life for the sheep. My sheep hear My voice, and I know them, and they follow Me."

PRECIOUS BLOOD CATHOLIC CHURCH
Culpeper, VA

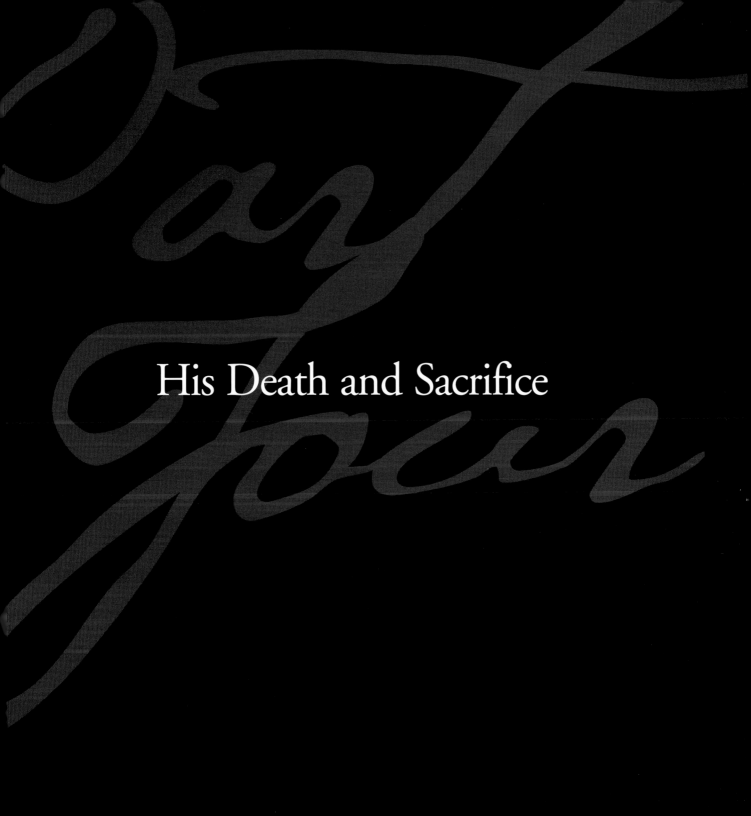

His Death and Sacrifice

JESUS IS TRANSFIGURED IN GLORY

MATTHEW 17:1–9

SS. PETER AND PAUL CATHOLIC CHURCH | *Cumberland, MD*

JESUS ACCEPTS AND APPRECIATES MARY'S ACT OF PROPHETIC OBEDIENCE

JOHN 12:1–8

Then, six days before the Passover, Jesus came to Bethany, where Lazarus was who had been dead, whom He had raised from the dead. There they made Him a supper; and Martha served, but Lazarus was one of those who sat at the table with Him. Then Mary took a pound of very costly oil of spikenard, anointed the feet of Jesus, and wiped his feet with her hair. And the house was filled with the fragrance of the oil. But one of His disciples, Judas Iscariot, Simon's son, who would betray Him, said, "Why was this fragrant oil not sold for three hundred denarii and given to the poor?" This he said, not that he cared for the poor, but because he was a thief, and had the money box; and he used to take what was put in it. But Jesus said, "Let her alone; she has kept this for the day of My burial. For the poor you have with you always, but Me you do not have always."

Jesus took Peter, James, and John his brother, led them up on a high mountain by themselves; and He was transfigured before them. His face shone like the sun, and His clothes became as white as the light. And behold, Moses and Elijah appeared to them, talking with Him. Then Peter answered and said to Jesus, "Lord, it is good for us to be here; if You wish, let us make here three tabernacles: one for You, one for Moses, and one for Elijah." While he was still speaking, behold, a bright cloud overshadowed them; and suddenly a voice came out of the cloud, saying, "This is My beloved Son, in whom I am well pleased. Hear Him!" And when the disciples heard it, they fell on their faces and were greatly afraid. But Jesus came and touched them and said, "Arise, and do not be afraid." When they had lifted up their eyes, they saw no one but Jesus only. Now as they came down from the mountain, Jesus commanded them, saying, "Tell the vision to no one until the Son of Man is risen from the dead."

WE CELEBRATE JESUS' TRIUMPHAL ENTRY INTO JERUSALEM ON PALM SUNDAY

MATTHEW 21:6–11

JUDAS BETRAYS JESUS FOR MONEY OFFERED BY THE PRIESTS TOWARDS HIS ARREST

MATTHEW 26:14–15, 17–18, 20–22, 25
Then one of the twelve called Judas Iscariot, went to the chief priests and said, "What are you willing to give me if I deliver Him to you?" And they counted out to him thirty pieces of silver. Now . . . the disciples came to Jesus, saying to Him, "Where do you want us to prepare for You to eat the Passover?" And He said, "Go into the city to a certain man, and say to him, 'The Teacher says, "My time is at hand; I will keep the Passover at your house with My disciples."'" When evening had come, He sat down with the twelve. Now as they were eating, He said, "Assuredly, I say to you, one of you will betray Me." And they were exceedingly sorrowful, and each of them began to say to Him, "Lord is it I?" Then Judas, who was betraying Him, answered and said, "Rabbi, is it I?" He said to him, "You have said it."

So the disciples went and did as Jesus commanded them. They brought the donkey and the colt, laid their clothes on them, and set Him on them. And a very great multitude spread their clothes on the road; others cut down branches from the trees and spread them on the road. Then the multitudes who went before and those who followed cried out, saying: "Hosanna to the Son of David; Blessed is He who comes in the name of the LORD. Hosanna in the highest!" And when He had come into Jerusalem, all the city was moved, saying, "Who is this?" So the multitudes said, "This is Jesus, the prophet from Nazareth of Galilee."

SAINT JOHN'S EPISCOPAL CHURCH, LAFAYETTE SQUARE
Washington, D.C.

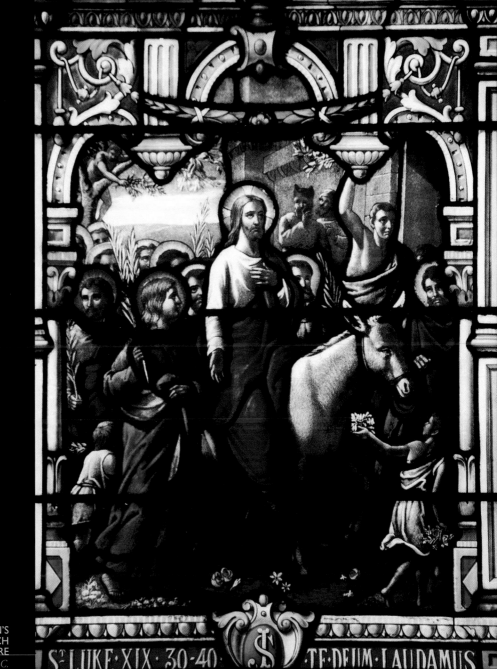

S⸱ LUKE · XIX · 30·40 · TE·DEUM·LAUDAMUS

WE MUST REMEMBER THAT JESUS' BODY WAS BROKEN FOR US

LUKE 22:14–16, 19

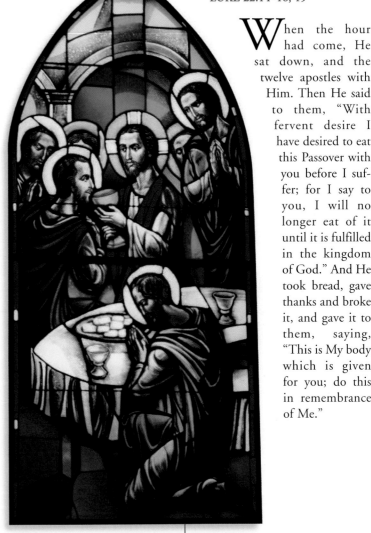

ST. MARY'S CHURCH [EPISCOPAL] | *Fleeton, VA*

AND HE SHED HIS BLOOD FOR OUR SINS AS A SEAL OF THE NEW COVENANT

MATTHEW 26:27–29

Then He took the cup, and gave thanks, and gave it to them, saying, "Drink from it, all of you. For this is My blood of the new covenant, which is shed for many for the remission of sins. But I say to you, I will not drink of this fruit of the vine from now on until that day when I drink it new with you in My Father's kingdom."

JOHN 13:26B–27, 31, 33–35

And having dipped the bread, He gave it to Judas Iscariot, the son of Simon. Now after the piece of bread, Satan entered him. Then Jesus said to him, "What you do, do quickly." So, when he had gone out, Jesus said, "Now the Son of Man is glorified, and God is glorified in Him. Little children, I shall be with you a little while longer. You will seek Me; and as I said to the Jews, 'Where I am going, you cannot come,' so now I say to you. A new commandment I give to you, that you love one another; as I have loved you, that you also love one another. By this all will know that you are My disciples, if you have love for one another."

When the hour had come, He sat down, and the twelve apostles with Him. Then He said to them, "With fervent desire I have desired to eat this Passover with you before I suffer; for I say to you, I will no longer eat of it until it is fulfilled in the kingdom of God." And He took bread, gave thanks and broke it, and gave it to them, saying, "This is My body which is given for you; do this in remembrance of Me."

ST. FRANCIS
OF ASSISI
CATHOLIC
CHURCH
Brainerd, MN

AND JESUS, MODELING SERVANTHOOD, WASHES PETER'S FEET

JOHN 13:2, 4–6A, 8-9, 12A, 14–17

CHAPEL AT THE CHURCH OF THE REDEEMER [EPISCOPAL]
Baltimore, MD

JESUS' WORDS OF FAREWELL TO HIS DISCIPLES

JOHN 14:19–20, 1,3;
15:13–14; 16:5, 7, 13–14

"A little while longer and the world will see Me no more, but you will see Me. Because I live, you will live also. At that day you will know that I am in My Father, and you in Me, and I in you. Let not your heart be troubled; you believe in God, believe also in Me. And if I go and prepare a place for you, I will come again and receive you to Myself; that where I am, there you may be also. Greater love has no one than this, than to lay down one's life for his friends. You are my friends if you do whatever I command you. But now I go away to Him who sent Me . . . nevertheless I tell you the truth. It is to your advantage that I go away; for if I do not go away, the Helper will not come to you; but if I depart, I will send Him to you. When He, the Spirit of truth, has come, He will guide you into all truth; for He will not speak on His own authority, but . . . He will glorify Me, for He will take of what is Mine and declare it to you."

And supper being ended, the devil having already put it into the heart of Judas Iscariot, Simon's son, to betray Him, Jesus . . . rose from supper . . . took a towel and . . . poured water into a basin and began to wash the disciples' feet, and to wipe them with the towel . . . Then He came to Simon Peter. And Peter said to Him, "You shall never wash my feet!" Jesus answered him, "If I do not wash you, you have no part with Me." Simon Peter said to Him, "Lord, not my feet only, but also my hands and my head!" So when He had washed their feet . . . He said to them, "If I then, your Lord and Teacher, have washed your feet, you also ought to wash one another's feet. For I have given you an example, that you should do as I have done to you. Most assuredly, I say to you, a servant is not greater than his master; nor is he who is sent greater than he who sent him. If you know these things, blessed are you if you do them."

IN GREAT SORROW, JESUS PRAYS TO HIS FATHER IN THE GARDEN OF GETHSEMANE

AN ANGEL COMFORTS JESUS IN HIS AGONY

LUKE 22:43–46

Then an angel appeared to Him from heaven, strengthening Him. And being in agony, He prayed more earnestly. Then His sweat became like great drops of blood falling down to the ground. When He rose up from prayer, and had come to His disciples, He found them sleeping from sorrow. Then He said to them, "Why do you sleep? Rise up and pray, lest you enter into temptation."

MATTHEW 26:44–45

So He left them, went away again, and prayed the third time, saying the same words. Then He came to His disciples and said to them, "Are you still sleeping and resting? Behold, the hour is at hand, and the Son of Man is being betrayed into the hands of sinners."

MATTHEW 26:36–40, 44A

Then Jesus came with them to a place called Gethsemane, and said to the disciples, "Sit here while I go and pray over there." And He took with Him Peter and the two sons of Zebedee, and He began to be sorrowful and deeply distressed. Then He said to them, "My soul is exceedingly sorrowful, even unto death. Stay here and watch with Me." He went a little farther and fell on His face, and prayed, saying, "O My Father, if it is possible, let this cup pass from Me; nevertheless, not as I will, but as You will." Then He came to the disciples and found them sleeping, and said to Peter, "What? Could you not watch with me one hour?" So He left them, went away again, and prayed . . .

ST. PAUL'S CATHOLIC CHURCH
Portsmouth, VA

JESUS PREDICTS THAT PETER WILL DENY KNOWING HIM

AND LATER, AFTER JESUS IS ARRESTED, PETER DENIES KNOWING HIM THREE TIMES!

MATTHEW 26:35
Peter said to Him, "Even if I have to die with You, I will not deny You!" And so said all the disciples.

LUKE 22:31–32
And the Lord said, "Simon, Simon! Indeed, Satan has asked for you, that he may sift you as wheat. But I have prayed for you, that your faith should not fail; and when you have returned to Me, strengthen your brethren."

MATTHEW 26:69–75
Now Peter sat outside in the courtyard. And a servant girl came to him, saying, "You also were with Jesus of Galilee." But he denied it before them all, saying, "I do not know what you are saying." And when he had gone out to the gateway, another girl saw him and said to those who were there, "This fellow also was with Jesus of Nazareth." But again he denied with an oath, "I do not know the Man!" And a little later those who stood by came up and said to Peter, "Surely you also are one of them, for your speech betrays you." Then he began to curse and swear, saying, "I do not know the Man!" Immediately a rooster crowed. And Peter remembered the word of Jesus who had said to him, "Before the rooster crows, you will deny Me three times." So he went out and wept bitterly.

MATTHEW 26:31–34

Then Jesus said to them, "All of you will be made to stumble because of Me this night, for it is written: 'I will strike the Shepherd, and the sheep of the flock will be scattered.' But after I have been raised, I will go before you to Galilee." Peter answered and said to Him, "Even if all are made to stumble because of You, I will never be made to stumble." Jesus said to him, "Assuredly, I say to you that this night, before the rooster crows, you will deny Me three times."

BASILICA OF THE NATIONAL SHRINE OF THE IMMACULATE CONCEPTION
Washington, D.C.

FROM THE BRONZE
DOOR TO ST. PETER
EN GALLICANTU,
Jerusalem, Israel

HE IS CAPTURED AND LED AWAY

JUDAS BETRAYS JESUS WITH A KISS

JOHN 18:2–3

And Judas, who betrayed Him, also knew the place; for Jesus often met there with His disciples. Then Judas, having received a detachment of troops, and officers from the chief priests and Pharisees, came there with lanterns, torches, and weapons.

LUKE 22:47–48, 52–53

Behold, a multitude; and he who was called Judas . . . went before them and drew near to Jesus to kiss Him.

THE CHURCH OF ALL NATIONS | *Jerusalem, Israel*

JOHN 18:4, 6, 12–13

Jesus therefore, knowing all things that would come upon Him, went forward and said to them, "Whom are you seeking?" They answered Him, "Jesus of Nazareth." Jesus said to them, "I am He." Now when He said, "I am He," they drew back and fell to the ground. Then the detachment of troops and the captain and the officers of the Jews arrested Jesus and bound Him. And they led him away to Annas first, for he was the father-in-law of Caiaphas who was high priest that year.

But Jesus said to him, "Judas, are you betraying the Son of Man with a kiss?" Then Jesus said to the chief priests, captains of the temple, and the elders who had come to Him, "Have you come out, as against a robber, with swords and clubs? When I was with you daily in the temple, you did not try to seize Me. But this is your hour, and the power of darkness."

THE TESTIMONY OF JESUS—
MOCKED AND SCORNED BY SOLDIERS

PILATE, THE ROMAN GOVERNOR OF JUDEA, PRONOUNCES HIM TO BE INNOCENT AND RELEASED

LUKE 23:1–2, 13–14, 16

Then the whole multitude of them arose and led Him to Pilate. And they began to accuse Him, saying, "We found this fellow perverting the nation, and forbidding to pay taxes to Caesar, saying, that He himself is Christ, a King." Then Pilate, when he had called together the chief priests, the rulers, and the people, said to them . . . "I have found no fault in this man concerning those things of which you accuse Him; I will therefore chastise Him and release Him."

Now the men who held Jesus mocked Him and beat Him. As soon as it was day, the elders of the people, both chief priests and scribes, came together and led Him into their council, saying, "If You are the Christ, tell us." But He said to them, "If I tell you, you will by no means believe. And if I also ask you, you will by no means answer Me or let Me go. Hereafter the Son of Man will sit on the right hand of the power of God." Then they all said, "Are you then the Son of God?" So He said to them, "You rightly say that I am." And they said, "What further testimony do we need?"

MATTHEW 27:27–30 & JOHN 19:5

Then the soldiers of the governor took Jesus into the Praetorium and gathered the whole garrison around Him. And they stripped Him and put a scarlet robe on Him. When they had twisted a crown of thorns, they put it on His head, and a reed in His right hand. And they bowed the knee before Him and mocked Him, saying, "Hail, King of the Jews!" Then they spat on Him, and took the reed and struck Him on the head. Then Jesus came out, wearing the crown of thorns and the . . . robe. And Pilate said to them, "Behold the Man!"

THE VIRGINIA THEOLOGICAL SEMINARY CHAPEL
Alexandria, VA

Pilate passes Judgment and Jesus is Led out to be Whipped and Crucified

A murderer released; Jesus condemned

MARK 14:1A; 15:6-7, 9-11, 15

It was the Passover and the Feast of Unleavened Bread. Now at the feast he was accustomed to releasing one prisoner to them, whomever they requested. And there was one named Barabbas, who was chained with his fellow rebels; they had committed murder in the rebellion. But Pilate answered them, saying, "Do you want me to release to you the King of the Jews?" For he knew that the chief priests had handed Him over because of envy. But the chief priests stirred up the crowd, so that he should rather release Barabbas to them. So Pilate, wanting to gratify the crowd, released Barabbas to them; and he delivered Jesus, after he had scourged Him, to be crucified.

But all the people and priests prevail, shouting that He be put to death

LUKE 23:5A, 18A, 20–21

But they were the more fierce, saying, "He stirs up the people . . ." And they all cried out at once, saying, "Away with this man . . ." Pilate, therefore, wishing to release Jesus, again called out to them. But they shouted, saying, "Crucify Him, crucify Him!"

MATTHEW 27:23A, 24–25

Then the governor said, "Why, what evil has He done?" When Pilate saw that he could not prevail at all, but rather that a tumult was rising . . . washed his hands before the multitude, saying, "I am innocent of the blood of this just Person. You see to it." And all the people answered and said, "His blood be on us and on our children."

ST. STEPHEN AND THE GOOD SHEPHERD EPISCOPAL CHURCH
Rocky Bar, VA

TO THE GREATER GLORY OF GOD
IN LOVING MEMORY OF ALL RECTORS OF CHRIST CHURCH

Simon, from Cyrene in Africa, is asked to carry the cross for Jesus

LUKE 23:26–28

Now as they led Him away, they laid hold of a certain man, Simon a Cyrenian, who was coming from the country, and on him they laid the cross that he might bear it after Jesus. And a great multitude of the people followed Him, and women who also mourned and lamented Him. But Jesus, turning to them, said, "Daughters of Jerusalem, do not weep for Me, but weep for yourselves and for your children."

PSALM 22:1-2A, 12-19

My God, My God, why have You forsaken Me? Why are you so far from helping Me, and from the words of My groaning? O My God, I cry in the daytime, but You do not hear. Many bulls have surrounded Me . . . they gape at Me with their mouths like a raging and roaring lion. I am poured out like water, and all of My bones are out of joint; My heart is like wax; it has melted within Me. My strength is dried up like a potsherd, and My tongue clings to My jaws; You have brought Me to the dust of death. For dogs have surrounded Me; the congregation of the wicked has enclosed Me. They pierced My hands and My feet; I can count all My bones. They look and stare at Me. They divide My garments among them, and for My clothing they cast lots. But You, O LORD, do not be far from Me; O My Strength, hasten to help ME!

ST. THERESA OF AVILA
CHURCH [CATHOLIC]
Washington, D.C.

Jesus' last words as He dies, hanging on a cross

LUKE 23:33–35, 46B; MATTHEW 27:37, 45–46; & JOHN 19:30B

God lays our sins on Jesus: our sacrificial Lamb

ISAIAH 53:12B, 3–8A, 10A
[A PROPHET'S TESTIMONY.]

He poured out His soul until death, and was numbered with our transgressors . . . He is despised and rejected by men, a Man of sorrows and acquainted with grief. And we hid, as it were, our faces from Him; He was despised, and we did not esteem Him. Surely He has borne our griefs and carried our sorrows; yet we esteemed Him stricken, smitten by God, and afflicted. But he was wounded for our transgressions, He was bruised for our iniquities; the chastisement for our peace was upon Him, and by His stripes we are healed. All we like sheep have gone astray; we have turned, every one, to his own way; and the LORD has laid on Him the iniquity of us all. He was oppressed and He was afflicted, yet He opened not His mouth; He was led as a lamb to the slaughter, and as a sheep before its shearers is silent, so He opened not His mouth. He was taken from prison and from judgment . . . yet it pleased the LORD to bruise Him; He has put Him to grief.

And when they had come to the place called Calvary, there they crucified Him, and the criminals, one on the right hand and the other on the left. Then Jesus said, "Father, forgive them, for they do not know what they do." And they divided His garments and cast lots. And the people stood looking on. But even the rulers with them sneered, saying, "He saved others; let Him save Himself if He is the Christ, the chosen of God." And they put up over His head the accusation written against Him, "THIS IS JESUS THE KING OF THE JEWS." Now from the sixth hour until the ninth hour there was darkness over all the land. And about the ninth hour Jesus cried out with a loud voice, saying . . . "My God, My God, why have You forsaken Me? Father, into Your hands I commit My spirit.' It is finished!" And bowing His head, He gave up His spirit.

MATTHEW 27:54

So when the centurion and those with him, who were guarding Jesus, saw the earthquake and the things that had happened, they feared greatly, saying, "Truly this was the Son of God!"

ST. MARY'S CATHOLIC CHURCH
Fredericksburg, VA

THE BURIAL OF JESUS

MARK 15:42–46

Now when evening had come . . . the day before the Sabbath, Joseph of Arimathea, a prominent council member, who was himself waiting for the kingdom of God, coming and taking courage, went in to Pilate and asked for the body of Jesus. Pilate marveled that He was already dead; and summoning the centurion, he asked him if He had been dead for some time. So when he found out from the centurion, he granted the body to Joseph. Then he brought fine linen, took Him down, and wrapped Him in the linen. And he laid Him in a tomb which had been hewn out of the rock, and rolled a stone against the door of the tomb.

DEEP SORROW HAS PIERCED THE HEART OF MARY, THE MOTHER OF JESUS

JOHN 19:25A, 31–36A
& LUKE 23:47–49

Now there stood by the cross of Jesus His mother and . . . when the centurion saw what had happened, he glorified God, saying, "Certainly this was a righteous Man!" And the whole crowd who came together to that sight, seeing what had been done, beat their breasts and returned. But all His acquaintances, and the women who followed Him from Galilee, stood at a distance, watching these things. Because it was the Preparation Day, that the bodies should not remain on the cross on the Sabbath . . . the soldiers came and broke the legs . . . but when they came to Jesus and saw that He was already dead, . . . one pierced . . . His side with a spear, and immediately blood and water came out. And he who has seen has testified . . . so that you may believe. For these things were done that the Scripture might be fulfilled.

ISAIAH 53:8B–9

For He was cut off from the land of the living; for the transgressions of My people He was stricken. And they made His grave with the wicked—but with the rich at His death, because He had done no violence, nor was any deceit in His mouth.

CATHEDRAL OF SAINT MATTHEW
THE APOSTLE [CATHOLIC]
Washington, D.C.

THERE LAID THEY JESUS

JOHN 15:9, 13; 10:11
As the Father loved Me, I also have loved you; abide in
My love. Greater love has no one than this, than to lay
down one's life for his friends. I am the good shepherd.
The good shepherd gives His life for the sheep.

LUKE 13:34
[Jesus laments,] O Jerusalem, Jerusalem, the one who
kills the prophets and stones those who are sent to her!
How often I wanted to gather your children together,
as a hen gathers her brood under her wings, but you
were not willing!

ISAIAH 53:5A
He was wounded for our transgressions,
He was bruised for our iniquities . . .

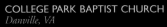

He Lives!

BEALE MEMORIAL
BAPTIST CHURCH
Tappahannock, VA

JESUS RISES OUT OF THE TOMB

MATTHEW 27:62–66; 28:1–4

On the next day . . . the chief priests and Pharisees gathered together to Pilate, saying, "Sir, we remember, while He was still alive, how that deceiver said, 'After three days I will rise.' Therefore command that the tomb be made secure until the third day, lest His disciples come by night and steal Him away, and say to the people, 'He has risen from the dead.' So the last deception will be worse than the first." Pilate said to them, "You have a guard; go your way, make it as secure as you know how." So they went and made the tomb secure, sealing the stone and setting the guard. Now after the Sabbath, as the first day of the week began to dawn . . . there was a great earthquake; for an angel of the Lord descended from heaven, and came and rolled back the stone from the door, and sat on it. His countenance was like lightning, and his clothing as white as snow. And the guards shook for fear of him, and became like dead men.

ST. JAMES'S EPISCOPAL CHURCH
Richmond, VA

"HE IS NOT HERE; FOR HE IS RISEN!"

MARK 16:1–4 &
MATTHEW 28:2B, 5–6A

Now when the Sabbath was past, Mary Magdalene, Mary the mother of James, and Salome bought spices, that they might come and anoint Him. Very early in the morning, on the first day of the week, they came to the tomb when the sun had risen. And they said among themselves, "Who will roll away the stone from the door of the tomb for us?" But when they looked up, they saw that the stone had been rolled away—for it was very large . . . for an angel of the Lord . . . rolled back the stone . . . and said to the women, "Do not be afraid, for I know that you seek Jesus who was crucified. He is not here; for he is risen . . ."

SAINT PAUL'S
EPISCOPAL
CHURCH
Norfolk, VA

THE WOMEN ARE ASTOUNDED AND JOYFUL, YET FEARFUL TO SEE THE TOMB EMPTY

MATTHEW 28:5A, 6B–8
& LUKE 24:5–8, 11–12

But the angel answered and said to the women, "Come, see the place where the Lord lay." Then, as they were afraid and bowed their faces to the earth, they said to them, "Why do you seek the living among the dead? He is not here, but is risen! Remember how He spoke to you when He was still in Galilee, saying, 'The Son of Man must be delivered into the hands of sinful men, and be crucified, and the third day rise again.'" And they remembered His words. "And go quickly and tell His disciples that He is risen from the dead, and indeed He is going before you into Galilee; there you will see Him. Behold, I have told you." So they went out quickly from the tomb with fear and great joy, and ran to bring His disciples word. And their words seemed to them like idle tales, and they did not believe them. But Peter arose and ran to the tomb; and stooping down, he saw the linen cloths lying by themselves; and he departed, marveling to himself at what had happened.

EMMANUEL EPISCOPAL CHURCH | *Chatham, VA*

JESUS APPEARS FIRST TO MARY MAGDALENE AND CONSOLES HER

JOHN 20:11–18

But Mary stood outside by the tomb weeping, and as she wept she stooped down and looked into the tomb. And she saw two angels in white sitting, one at the head and the other at the feet, where the body of Jesus had lain. Then they said to her, "Woman, why are you weeping?" She said to them, "Because they have taken away my Lord, and I do not know where they have laid Him." Now when she had said this, she turned around and saw Jesus standing there, and did not know that it was Jesus. Jesus said to her, "Woman, are you weeping? Whom are you seeking?" She, supposing Him to be the gardener, said to Him, "Sir, if You have carried Him away, tell me where You have laid Him, and I will take Him away." Jesus said to her, "Mary!" She turned and said to Him, "Rabboni!" (which is to say, Teacher). Jesus said to her, "Do not cling to Me, for I have not yet ascended to My Father; but go to My brethren and say to them, 'I am ascending to My Father and your Father, and to My God and your God.'" Mary Magdalene came and told the disciples that she had seen the Lord, and that He had spoken these things to her.

JESUS TALKS TO TWO MEN ON THE ROAD TO EMMAUS

LUKE 24:13–21A

Now behold, two of them were traveling that same day to a village called Emmaus, which was seven miles from Jerusalem. And they talked together of all these things which had happened. So it was, while they conversed and reasoned, that Jesus Himself drew near and went with them. But their eyes were restrained, so that they did not know Him. And He said to them, "What kind of conversation is this that you have with one another as you walk and are sad?" Then the one whose name was Cleopas answered and said to Him, "Are You the only stranger in Jerusalem, and have You not known the things which happened . . . concerning Jesus of Nazareth, who was a Prophet mighty in deed and word before God . . . and how the chief priests and our rulers delivered Him to be condemned to death, and crucified Him? But we were hoping that it was He who was going to redeem Israel."

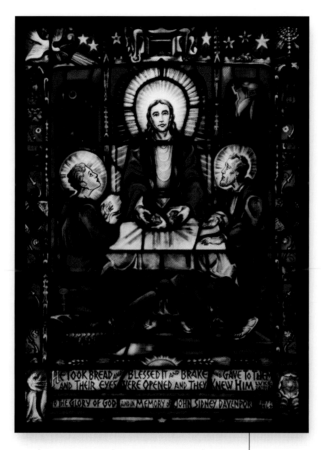

GRACE AND HOLY TRINITY EPISCOPAL CHURCH | *Richmond, VA*

AND THEY DID NOT RECOGNIZE HIM UNTIL AFTER HE BROKE THE BREAD AT SUPPER

LUKE 24:25–32

Then He said to them, "O foolish ones, and slow of heart to believe in all that the prophets have spoken! Ought not the Christ to have suffered these things and to enter into His glory?" And beginning at Moses and all the Prophets, He expounded to them in all the Scriptures the things concerning Himself. Then they drew near to the village where they were going, and He indicated that He would have gone farther. But they constrained Him, saying, "Abide with us, for it is toward evening . . . " And He went in to stay with them. Now it came to pass, as He sat at the table with them, that He took bread, blessed and broke it, and gave it to them. Then their eyes were opened and they knew Him; and He vanished from their sight. And they said to one another, "Did not our heart burn within us while He talked with us on the road, and while He opened the Scriptures to us?"

HANDLE ME AND SEE THAT I AM ALIVE!

LUKE 24:33–43

So they rose up that very hour and returned to Jerusalem, and found the eleven and those who were with them gathered together, saying, "The Lord is risen indeed, and has appeared to Simon!" And they told about the things that had happened on the road, and how He was known to them in the breaking of bread. Now as they said these things, Jesus Himself stood in the midst of them, and said to them, "Peace to you." But they were terrified and frightened, and supposed they had seen a spirit. And He said to them, "Why are you troubled? And why do doubts arise in your hearts? Behold My hands and My feet, that it is I Myself. Handle Me and see, for a spirit does not have flesh and bones as you see I have." When He had said this, He showed them His hands and His feet. But while they still did not believe for joy, and marveled, He said to them, "Have you any food here?" So they gave Him a piece of a broiled fish and some honeycomb. And He took it and ate in their presence.

THOMAS GETS PROOF THAT JESUS IS ALIVE AND THEN CRIES, "MY LORD AND MY GOD!"

JOHN 20:24–29

Now Thomas, called the Twin, one of the twelve, was not with them when Jesus came. The other disciples therefore said to him, "We have seen the Lord." So he said to them, "Unless I see in His hands the print of the nails . . . and put my hand into His side, I will not believe." And after eight days His disciples were again inside, and Thomas with them. Jesus came, the doors being shut, and stood in the midst, and said, "Peace to you!" Then He said to Thomas, "Reach your finger here, and look at My hands; and reach your hand here, and put it into

THE CHAPEL OF THE RESURRECTION
IN THE WASHINGTON NATIONAL CATHEDRAL | *Washington, D.C.*

My side. Do not be unbelieving, but believing." And Thomas answered and said to Him, "My Lord and my God!" Jesus said to him, "Thomas, because you have seen Me, you have believed. Blessed are those who have not seen and yet have believed."

A BIG FISH STORY AND BREAKFAST WITH THE LORD

JOHN 21:1–7A, 9, 12–13

After these things Jesus showed Himself again to the disciples at the Sea of Tiberias, and in this way He showed Himself: . . . His disciples were together; Simon Peter said to them, "I am going fishing." They said to him, "We are going with you also." They went out . . . and that night they caught nothing. But when the morning had now come, Jesus stood on the shore; yet the disciples did not know that it was Jesus. Then Jesus said to them, "Children, have you any food?" They answered Him, "No." And He said to them, "Cast the net on the right side of the boat, and you will find some." So they cast, and now they were not able to draw it in because of the multitude of fish. Therefore that disciple whom Jesus loved said to Peter, "It is the Lord!" Then, as soon as they had come to land, they saw a fire of coals there, and fish laid on it, and bread. Jesus said to them, "Come and eat breakfast." Yet none of the disciples dared ask Him, "Who are You?"—knowing that it was the Lord. Jesus then came and took the bread and gave it to them, and likewise the fish.

SCRIPTURES OF THE OLD TESTAMENT MUST BE FULFILLED

LUKE 24:44–49

Then He said to them, "These are the words which I spoke to you while I was still with you, that all things must be fulfilled which were written in the Law of Moses and the Prophets and the Psalms concerning Me." And He opened their understanding, that they might comprehend the Scriptures. Then He said to them, "Thus it is written, and thus it was necessary for the Christ to suffer and to rise from the dead the third day, and that repentance and remission of sins should be preached in His name to all nations, beginning at Jerusalem. And you are witnesses of these things. Behold, I send the Promise of My Father upon you; but tarry in the city of Jerusalem until you are endued with power from on high."

THE VIRGINIA THEOLOGICAL SEMINARY CHAPEL
Alexandria, VA

IC XC

SAINT NICHOLAS
CATHEDRAL,
ORTHODOX
CHURCH
Washington, D.C.

JESUS COMMISSIONS HIS DISCIPLES

MATTHEW 28:10, 17–20

Then Jesus said to them, "Do not be afraid. Go and tell My brethren to go to Galilee, and there they will see Me." When they saw Him, they worshiped Him; but some doubted. And Jesus came and spoke to them, saying, "All authority has been given to Me in heaven and on earth. Go therefore and make disciples of all the nations, baptizing them in the name of the Father and of the Son and of the Holy Spirit, teaching them to observe all things that I have commanded you; and lo, I am with you always, even to the end of the age." Amen.

ST. ANTHONY OF PADUA
CATHOLIC CHURCH
Minneapolis, MN

JESUS ASCENDS INTO HEAVEN

LUKE 24:50–53 & ACTS 1:9B–11

And He led them out as far as Bethany, and He lifted up His hands and blessed them. Now it came to pass, while He blessed them, that He was parted from them and carried up into heaven. He was taken up, and a cloud received Him out of their sight. And while they looked steadfastly toward heaven as He went up, behold, two men stood by them in white apparel, who also said, "Men of Galilee, why do you stand gazing up into heaven? This same Jesus, who was taken up from you into heaven, will so come in like manner as you saw Him go into heaven." And they worshiped Him, and returned to Jerusalem with great joy, and were continually in the temple praising and blessing God. Amen.

WESTMINSTER
PRESBYTERIAN
CHURCH
Wilmington, DE

The church and the world are all under Jesus' authority

EPHESIANS 1:17A, 20B–23

The God of our Lord Jesus Christ . . . raised Him from the dead and seated Him at His right hand in the heavenly places, far above all principality and power and might and dominion, and every name that is named, not only in this age but also in that which is to come. And He put all things under His feet, and gave Him to be head over all things to the church, which is His body, the fullness of Him who fills all in all.

REVELATION 11:15

And there were loud voices in heaven, saying, "The kingdoms of this world have become the kingdoms of our Lord and of His Christ, and He shall reign forever and forever!"

JESUS, OUR LORD AND KING, WORTHY OF ALL GLORY, HONOR, AND POWER

REVELATION 4:2, 10–11; 5:5A; 19:16

Immediately I was in the Spirit; and behold, a throne set in heaven, and One sat on the throne. [T]wenty-four elders fall down before Him who sits on the throne and worship Him who lives forever and ever, and cast their crowns before the throne, saying, "You are worthy, O Lord, to receive glory and honor and power; for You created all things, and by Your will they exist and were created." But one of the elders said to me . . . "Behold, the Lion of the tribe of Judah, the Root of David, has prevailed . . . and He has on His robe and on His thigh a name written, **KING OF KINGS AND LORD OF LORDS.**"

SAINTS CONSTANTINE AND HELEN GREEK ORTHODOX CHURCH
Washington, D.C.

ANNANDA
UNITED
METHODIS
CHURCH,

JOB 19:25A

"For I know that my Redeemer lives . . ."

The Invitation

JESUS KNOCKS ON THE DOOR OF MY HEART AND I WILL ANSWER

REVELATION 3:20

"Behold, I stand at the door and knock. If anyone hears My voice and opens the door, I will come in to him and dine with him, and he with Me."

HE OFFERS ME HIS LOVE AND COMFORT

JOHN 10:14, 28–29; 15:9

"I am the good shepherd; and I know My sheep, and am known by My own. And I give them eternal life, and they shall never perish . . . My Father, who has given them to Me, is greater than all; and no one is able to snatch them out of My Father's hand. As the Father loved Me, I also have loved you; abide in My love."

ISAIAH 40:11

He will feed His flock like a shepherd; He will gather the lambs with His arm, and carry them in His bosom . . .

MATTHEW 11:28–30

"Come to Me, all you who labor and are heavy laden, and I will give you rest. Take My yoke upon you and learn from Me, for I am gentle and lowly in heart, and you will find rest for your souls. For My yoke is easy and My burden is light."

JOHN 6:35; 8:12

And Jesus said to them, "I am the bread of life. He who comes to Me shall never hunger, and he who believes in Me shall never thirst. I am the light of the world. He who follows Me shall not walk in darkness, but have the light of life."

JOHN 10:9

"I am the door. If anyone enters by Me, he will be saved, and will go in and out and find pasture."

ST. JAMES' EPISCOPAL CHURCH
Louisa, VA

TRINITY
EPISCOPAL
CHURCH
Rocky Mount, VA

I WILL BELIEVE AND SAY THAT JESUS IS MY LORD AND THE SON OF GOD

BETHLEHEM CHRISTIAN CHURCH | *Suffolk, VA*

I MUST REPENT, CHANGE MY WAYS, AND BE BAPTIZED

ACTS 2:14A, 29A, 32–33A, 36–38, 41

But Peter, standing up with the eleven, raised his voice and said to them, "Men and brethren, let me speak freely to you . . . This Jesus God has raised up, of which we all are witnesses . . . being exalted to the right hand of God . . . let all the house of Israel know assuredly that God has made this Jesus, whom you crucified, both Lord and Christ." Now when they heard this, they were cut to the heart, and said to Peter and the rest of the apostles, "Men and brethren, what shall we do?" Then Peter said to them, "Repent, and let every one of you be baptized in the name of Jesus Christ for the remission of sins; and you shall receive the gift of the Holy Spirit." Then those who gladly received his word were baptized; and that day about three thousand souls were added to them.

JOHN 3:16–17

"For God so loved the world that He gave His only begotten Son, that whoever believes in Him should not perish but have everlasting life. For God did not send His Son into the world to condemn the world, but that the world through Him might be saved."

MARK 10:45

"For even the Son of Man did not come to be served, but to serve, and to give His life a ransom for many."

MATTHEW 18:11

"For the Son of Man has come to save that which was lost."

ROMANS 10:9–10

"If you confess with your mouth the Lord Jesus and believe in your heart that God has raised Him from the dead, you will be saved. For with the heart one believes unto righteousness, and with the mouth confession is made unto salvation."

JOEL 2:32A

"And it shall come to pass that whoever calls on the name of the LORD shall be saved."

PHILIPPIANS 4:13

"I can do all things through Christ who strengthens me."

SAINT JOHN
THE BAPTIST
ROMAN
CATHOLIC
CHURCH
Front Royal, VA

Under the law, death is the penalty for sin, but praise God . . .

ROMANS 6:23; 3:23

Jesus has set me free!

1 CORINTHIANS 15:56–57
The sting of death is sin, and the strength of sin is the law. But thanks be to God, who gives us the victory through our Lord Jesus Christ.

JOHN 8:31–32, 36; 3:21
Then Jesus said to those Jews who believed Him, "If you abide in My word, you are My disciples indeed. And you shall know the truth, and the truth shall make you free. Therefore if the Son makes you free, you shall be free indeed . . . But he who does the truth comes to the light, that his deeds may be clearly seen, that they have been done in God."

ACTS 3:19 & PSALM 103:12
"Repent therefore and be converted, that your sins may be blotted out, so that times of refreshing may come from the presence of the Lord." As far as the east is from the west, so far has He removed our transgressions from us.

ROMANS 6:18
And having been set free from sin, you became slaves of righteousness.

For the wages of sin is death, but the gift of God is eternal life in Christ Jesus our Lord. For all have sinned and fall short of the glory of God.

ROMANS 14:12
So then each of us shall give account of himself to God.

ROMANS 5:8–9; 6:4A, 8B, 14; 14:8
But God demonstrates His own love toward us, in that while we were still sinners, Christ died for us. Much more then, having now been justified by His blood, we shall be saved from wrath through Him. Therefore we were buried with Him through baptism into death . . . we believe that we shall also live with Him . . . For sin shall not have dominion over you, for you are not under law but under grace. For if we live, we live to the Lord; and if we die, we die to the Lord. Therefore, whether we live or die, we are the Lord's.

PSALM 50:15
Call upon Me in the day of trouble; I will deliver you and you shall glorify Me.

MEADE MEMORIAL EPISCOPAL CHURCH
Alexandria, VA

SAINT ALPHONSUS CHURCH [CATHOLIC] *Wheeling, WV*

I HAVE MADE WRONG CHOICES AND WILL ASK MY FATHER GOD TO FORGIVE MY SINS

I WILL FORGIVE OTHERS SO THAT MY FATHER WILL FORGIVE ME

JOHN 8:7B
[Jesus says], "He who is without sin among you, let him throw a stone at her first."

LUKE 11:4A
"And forgive us our sins, for we also forgive everyone who is indebted to us."

MATTHEW 18:21–22
Then Peter came to Him and said, "Lord, how often shall my brother sin against me, and I forgive him? Up to seven times?" Jesus said to him, "I do not say to you, up to seven times, but up to seventy times seven."

MATTHEW 6:14–15
"For if you forgive men their trespasses, your heavenly Father will also forgive you. But if you do not forgive men their trespasses, neither will your Father forgive your trespasses."

PSALM 136:1
O, give thanks to the LORD, for He is good! For His mercy endures forever.

FIRST BAPTIST CHURCH | *Martinsville, VA*

1 JOHN 1:8–9; 2:1
If we say that we have no sin, we deceive ourselves, and the truth is not in us. If we confess our sins, He is faithful and just to forgive us our sins and to cleanse us from all unrighteousness. My little children, these things I write to you, so that you may not sin. And if anyone sins, we have an Advocate with the Father, Jesus Christ the righteous.

ISAIAH 6:5A
So I said; "Woe is me, for I am undone! Because I am a man of unclean lips . . ."

LUKE 15:21
"And the son said to him, 'Father, I have sinned against heaven and in your sight, and am no longer worthy to be called your son.'"

PSALM 51:10, 2
Create in me a clean heart, O God, and renew a steadfast spirit within me. Wash me thoroughly from my iniquity and cleanse me from my sin.

I WILL CHOOSE A CHURCH HOME AND WILL SET ASIDE ONE DAY A WEEK TO WORSHIP

AND PRAISE GOD WITH MY FAMILY IN CHRIST

PRAISE YE THE LORD

SHILOH MISSIONARY BAPTIST CHURCH
Martinsville, VA

EXODUS 20:8–10A

"Remember the Sabbath day, to keep it holy. Six days you shall labor and do all your work, but the seventh day is the Sabbath of the LORD your God. In it you shall do no work."

MARK 11:17A

"Is it not written, 'My house shall be called a house of prayer for all nations?'"

PSALM 134:1–2

Behold, bless the LORD, all you servants of the LORD, who by night stand in the house of the LORD! Lift up your hands in the sanctuary, and bless the LORD.

1 PETER 5:1A, 2–3

The elders who are among you I exhort . . . shepherd the flock of God . . . serving as overseers, not by compulsion but willingly, not for dishonest gain, but eagerly; nor as being lords over those entrusted to you, but being examples to the flock.

PSALM 122:1

I was glad when they said to me, "Let us go into the house of the LORD."

PSALM 132:7, 9

Let us go into His tabernacle; let us worship at His footstool. Let Your priests be clothed with righteousness, and let Your saints shout for joy.

ISAIAH 57:15

For thus says the High and Lofty One who inhabits eternity, whose name is Holy: "I dwell in the high and holy place, with him who has a contrite and humble spirit . . ."

ISAIAH 58:13–14A

"If you turn away your foot from the Sabbath, from doing your pleasure on My holy day, and call the Sabbath a delight, the holy day of the LORD honorable, and shall honor Him, not doing your own ways . . . then you shall delight yourself in the LORD.

PSALM 148:1–3

Praise the LORD!
Praise the LORD from the heavens;
Praise Him in the heights!
Praise Him, all His angels;
Praise Him, all His hosts!
Praise Him, sun and moon;
Praise Him, all you stars of light!

PRAISE YE

IXΘYΣ

THE LORD
ALL HIS ANGELS
PRAISE YE HIM
SUN AND MOON
ALL YE STARS OF LIGHT
PSALM 148
IN HONOR OF MR AND MRS. J.A. KAVALGA AND FAMILY

TRINITY
LUTHERAN
CHURCH
Hagerstown, MD

I WILL SHARE THE LORD'S SUPPER WITH THE BODY OF CHRIST

LUKE 22:19

AND USE MY TALENTS TO SERVE AND BUILD UP THE CHURCH BODY

ROMANS 12:4–8, 10–13

For as we have many members in one body, but all the members do not have the same function, so we, being many, are one body in Christ, and individually members of one another. Having then gifts differing according to the grace that is given to us, let us use them: if prophecy, let us prophesy in proportion to our faith; or ministry, let us use it in our ministering; he who teaches, in teaching; he who exhorts, in exhortation; he who gives, with liberality; he who leads, with diligence; he who shows mercy, with cheerfulness. Be kindly affectionate to one another with brotherly love, in honor giving preference to one another; not lagging in diligence, fervent in spirit, serving the Lord; rejoicing in hope, patient in tribulation, continuing steadfastly in prayer; distributing to the needs of the saints, given to hospitality.

And He took bread, gave thanks and broke it, and gave it to them, saying, "This is My body which is given for you; do this in remembrance of Me."

MATTHEW 26:27–28

Then He took the cup, and gave thanks, and gave it to them, saying, "Drink from it, all of you. For this is My blood of the new covenant, which is shed for many for the remission of sins."

1 JOHN 1:7

But if we walk in the light as He is in the light, we have fellowship with one another, and the blood of Jesus Christ His Son cleanses us from all sin.

PSALM 133:1

Behold, how good and how pleasant it is for brethren to dwell together in unity!

ST. JAMES' EPISCOPAL CHURCH
Leesburg, VA

ST. MARGARET'S
EPISCOPAL CHURCH
Woodbridge, VA

AS I READ THE BIBLE, ITS AUTHOR SPEAKS TO ME

MY GOD IS SOVEREIGN AND I WILL TRUST IN HIM AS MY PROTECTIVE FATHER

PSALM 18:2
The LORD is my rock and my fortress and my deliverer; my God, my strength, in whom I will trust.

DEUTERONOMY 33:12
The beloved of the LORD shall dwell in safety by Him, Who shelters him all the day long; and he shall dwell between His shoulders.

1 CORINTHIANS 2:16A
For "who has known the mind of the LORD that he may instruct Him?"

1 JOHN 3:1A
Behold what manner of love the Father has bestowed on us, that we should be called children of God!

PSALM 70:4
Let all those who seek You rejoice and be glad in You; and let those who love Your salvation say continually, "Let God be magnified!"

2 CHRONICLES 26:5B
As long as he sought the LORD, God made him prosper.

PORT REPUBLIC
UNITED METHODIST
CHURCH
Port Republic, VA

2 TIMOTHY 3:16–17
All Scripture is given by inspiration of God, and is profitable for doctrine, for reproof, for correction, for instruction in righteousness, that the man of God may be complete, thoroughly equipped for every good work.

DEUTERONOMY 8:3B
"Man shall not live by bread alone; but man lives by every word that proceeds from the mouth of the LORD."

JOHN 1:1
In the beginning was the Word, and the Word was with God, and the Word was God.

JOHN 8:31–32
Then Jesus said to those Jews who believed Him, "If you abide in My word, you are My disciples indeed. And you shall know the truth, and the truth shall make you free."

PSALM 119:105
Your word is a lamp to my feet and a light to my path.

LUKE 11:28
"Blessed are those who hear the word of God and keep it!"

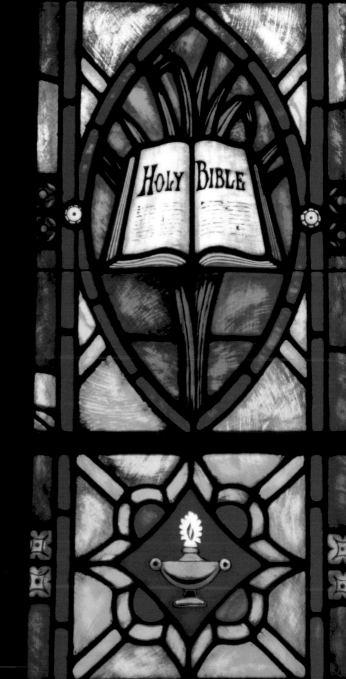

ST. JAMES CATHOLIC CHURCH
Charles Town, WV

MATTHEW 7:20

"Therefore by their fruits you will know them."

JOHN 12:24

"Most assuredly, I say to you, unless a grain of wheat falls into the ground and dies, it remains alone; but if it dies, it produces much grain."

SHILOH
MISSIONARY
BAPTIST
CHURCH
Cascade, VA

From Ashes to Flames

INNER CONVERSION

Lord, I am having trouble and I yearn to come to you as my Father

PSALM 143:6

I spread out my hands to You; my soul longs for You like a thirsty land.

PSALM 42:1–2A

As the deer pants for the water brooks, so pants my soul for You, O God. My soul thirsts for God, for the living God.

MARK 9:24B, 23, 5:36B

"Lord, I believe; help my unbelief!" Jesus said . . . "If you can believe, all things are possible to him who believes. Do not be afraid; only believe."

MATTHEW 18:2–4

Jesus called a little child to Him, set him in the midst of them, and said, "Assuredly, I say to you, unless you are converted and become as little children, you will by no means enter the kingdom of heaven. Therefore whoever humbles himself as this little child is the greatest in the kingdom of heaven."

ST. MARY MISSION
Tohatchi, NM

I will not look back but seek the life-giving streams of God in the desert

MATTHEW 9:9B

And He said to him, "Follow Me."

PSALM 63:1

O God, You are my God; early will I seek You; my soul thirsts for You; my flesh longs for You in a dry and thirsty land where there is no water.

MARK 6:31B

And He said to them, "Come aside by yourselves to a deserted place and rest awhile."

ISAIAH 43:16A, 18–19

Thus says the Lord, who makes a way . . . "Do not remember the former things, nor consider the things of old. Behold, I will do a new thing, now it shall spring forth . . . I will even make a road in the wilderness and rivers in the desert."

PSALM 23:1–3A

The Lord is my shepherd; I shall not want. He makes me to lie down in green pastures; He leads me beside the still waters. He restores my soul . . .

ST. ANNE'S
EPISCOPAL CHURCH
Annapolis, MD

I WILL PRAY TO RECEIVE THE HOLY SPIRIT

LUKE 3:16

John answered, saying to all, "I indeed baptize you with water; but One mightier than I is coming, whose sandal strap I am not worthy to loose. He will baptize you with the Holy Spirit and fire."

ACTS 8:17, 10:45–46

Then they laid hands on them, and they received the Holy Spirit. And those . . . were astonished . . . because the gift of the Holy Spirit had been poured out on the Gentiles also. For they heard them speak with tongues and magnify God.

JOHN 15:7

"If you abide in Me, and My words abide in you, you will ask what you desire, and it shall be done for you."

PRINCE OF PEACE LUTHERAN CHURCH | *Springfield, VA*

AND HE WILL COME AND MAKE HIS HOME IN MY HEART

JOEL 2:28

"And it shall come to pass . . . that I will pour out My Spirit on all flesh; your sons and your daughters shall prophesy, your old men shall dream dreams, your young men shall see visions."

ACTS 1:8

"You shall receive power when the Holy Spirit has come upon you; and you shall be witnesses to Me in Jerusalem . . . and to the end of the earth."

ACTS 2:1–4, 4:31

When the Day of Pentecost had fully come, they were all with one accord in one place. And suddenly there came a sound from heaven, as of a rushing mighty wind, and it filled the whole house where they were sitting. Then there appeared to them divided tongues, as of fire, and one sat upon each of them. And they were all filled with the Holy Spirit and began to speak with other tongues, as the Spirit gave them utterance. And when they had prayed, the place where they were assembled together was shaken . . . and they spoke the word of God with boldness.

ROMANS 8:14, 17

For as many as are led by the Spirit of God, these are the sons of God . . . and if children, then heirs—heirs of God and joint heirs with Christ, if indeed we suffer with Him, that we may also be glorified together.

THE WASHINGTON
NATIONAL CATHEDRAL
Washington, D.C.

THE HOLY SPIRIT IS A CONSUMING FIRE

EXODUS 13:21

A nd the LORD went before them by day in a pillar of cloud to lead the way, and by night in a pillar of fire to give them light.

1 KINGS 18:38A, 39

Then the fire of the LORD fell and consumed the burnt sacrifice, and the wood and the stones and the dust, and it licked up the water that was in the trench. Now when all the people saw it, they fell on their faces; and they said, "The LORD, He is God! The LORD, He is God!"

JOHN 16:7–11

"It is to your advantage that I go away; for if I do not go away, the Helper will not come to you . . . and when He has come, He will convict the world of sin, and of righteousness, and of judgment: of sin because they do not believe in Me; of righteousness, because I go to My Father and you see Me no more; of judgment, because the ruler of this world is judged."

1 THESSALONIANS 5:19

Do not quench the Spirit.

HEBREWS 12:29

For our God is a consuming fire.

SPENCERVILLE
SEVENTH-DAY
ADVENTIST CHURCH
Spencerville, MD

THE HOLY SPIRIT IS GENTLE

MATTHEW 3:16B

He saw the Spirit of God descending like a dove and alighting upon Him.

JOHN 14:15–18, 19B–20

"If you love Me, keep My commandments. And I will pray the Father, and He will give you another Helper, that He may abide with you forever—the Spirit of truth, whom the world cannot receive, because it neither sees Him nor knows Him . . . for He dwells with you and will be in you. I will not leave you orphans; I will come to you. Because I live, you will live also. At that day you will know that I am in My Father, and you in Me, and I in you."

1 JOHN 4:2

By this you know the Spirit of God: Every spirit that confesses that Jesus Christ has come in the flesh is of God.

GALATIANS 5:22–23A

But the fruit of the Spirit is love, joy, peace, long-suffering, kindness, goodness, faithfulness, gentleness, self-control.

IMMANUEL'S
CHURCH
Silver Spring, MD

THE HOLY SPIRIT WILL TEACH AND GUIDE ME IN THE WISDOM OF GOD

JOHN 16:13

"However, when He, the Spirit of Truth, has come, He will guide you into all truth; for He will not speak on His own authority, but whatever He hears He will speak; and He will tell you things to come."

1 CORINTHIANS 2:10B
For the Spirit searches all things, yes, the deep things of God.

1 CORINTHIANS 6:19–20
Do you not know that your body is the temple of the Holy Spirit who is in you, whom you have from God, and you are not your own? For you were bought at a price; therefore glorify God in your body and in your spirit, which are God's.

SEEK THE LORD ALWAYS —LIKE US HE IS A MAN OF SORROWS BUT A LORD OF JOY

PSALM 27:4
One thing I have desired of the LORD, that I will seek: that I may dwell in the house of the LORD all the days of my life, to behold the beauty of the LORD, and to inquire in His temple.

PSALM 34:8
O, taste and see that the LORD is good; blessed is the man who trusts in Him!

ISAIAH 53:3A, 4–5
He is despised and rejected by men, a Man of sorrows and acquainted with grief. Surely He has borne our griefs and carried our sorrows; yet we esteemed Him stricken, smitten by God, and afflicted. But He was wounded for our transgressions, He was bruised for our iniquities . . . and by His stripes we are healed.

NEHEMIAH 8:10B
"Do not sorrow, for the joy of the LORD is your strength."

ST. KATHERINE'S GREEK
ORTHODOX CHURCH
Falls Church, VA

JOHN 15:11
"These things I have spoken to you, that My joy may remain in you, and that your joy may be full."

JOHN 2:6–9A
Now there were . . . six waterpots of stone . . . containing twenty or thirty gallons apiece. Jesus said . . . "Fill the waterpots with water . . . draw some out now, and take it to the master of the feast;" the water that was made wine.

June 20th.
1823

George Oliver Conrad

Jan 23rd
1907

ASBURY UNITED
METHODIST
CHURCH
Harrisonburg, VA

LORD, HELP ME TO GIVE MY WORLDLY DESIRES, WEAKNESSES, AND BURDENS TO YOU

MATTHEW 16:24–27

Then Jesus said to His disciples, "If anyone desires to come after Me, let him deny himself, and take up his cross, and follow Me. For whoever desires to save his life will lose it, but whoever loses his life for My sake will find it. For what profit is it to a man if he gains the whole world, and loses his own soul? Or what will a man give in exchange for his soul? For the Son of Man will come and . . . He will reward each according to his works."

ROMANS 8:8; GALATIANS 5:16, 24

So then, those who are in the flesh cannot please God. I say then: Walk in the Spirit, and you shall not fulfill the lust of the flesh. And those who are Christ's have crucified the flesh with its passions and desires.

PSALM 73:23–24

Nevertheless I am continually with You; You hold me by my right hand. You will guide me with Your counsel, and afterward receive me to glory.

2 CORINTHIANS 5:7

For we walk by faith, not by sight.

ST. JAMES'S EPISCOPAL CHURCH
Richmond, VA

MY LIFE IS DIFFICULT, BUT I HAVE TO TRUST YOU, LORD, TO LEAD ME

MATTHEW 7:13–14

"Enter by the narrow gate; for wide is the gate and broad is the way that leads to destruction, and there are many who go in by it. Because narrow is the gate and difficult is the way which leads to life, and there are few who find it."

ISAIAH 30:21

Your ears shall hear a word behind you, saying, "This is the way, walk in it . . . "

PSALM 32:8

I will instruct you and teach you in the way you should go; I will guide you with My eye.

MATTHEW 5:16

"Let your light so shine before men, that they may see your good works and glorify your Father in heaven."

PSALM 62:8

Trust in Him at all times, you people; pour out your heart before Him; God is a refuge for us.

I WILL HOLD ON TO JESUS WITH ALL THAT I HAVE

REVELATION 3:19

"As many as I love, I rebuke and chasten. Therefore be zealous and repent."

1 PETER 5:8–9

Be sober, be vigilant; because your adversary the devil walks about like a roaring lion, seeking whom he may devour. Resist him, steadfast in the faith, knowing that the same sufferings are experienced by your brotherhood in the world.

PSALM 34:19

Many are the afflictions of the righteous, but the LORD delivers him out of them all.

JOB 2:10B

"Shall we indeed accept good from God, and shall we not accept adversity?"

ROMANS 8:38–39

For I am persuaded that neither death nor life . . . nor any other created thing, shall be able to separate us from the love of God which is in Jesus Christ our Lord.

1 CORINTHIANS 1:18

For the message of the cross is foolishness to those who are perishing, but to us who are being saved it is the power of God.

HE IS MY HEALER AND IN CHARGE OF MY LIFE

ST. JOHN'S UNITED
METHODIST CHURCH
Edinburg, VA

Courtesy of the artist,
James H. Clark

EXODUS 15:26B

"For I am the LORD who heals you."

PSALM 50:15

"Call upon Me in the day of trouble; I will deliver you, and you shall glorify Me."

JEREMIAH 29:11

"For I know the thoughts that I think toward you," says the LORD, "thoughts of peace and not of evil, to give you a future and a hope."

PSALM 25:4–7

Show me Your ways, O LORD; teach me Your paths. Lead me in Your truth and teach me, for You are the God of my salvation; on You I wait all the day. Remember, O LORD, Your tender mercies and your lovingkindnesses, for they are from of old. Do not remember the sins of my youth, nor my transgressions; according to Your mercy remember me, for Your goodness' sake, O LORD.

THE PRESENCE OF THE LORD IS MORE IMPORTANT THAN ANYTHING IN THE WORLD

2 CORINTHIANS 12:7–9, 10B

And lest I should be exalted above measure . . . a thorn in the flesh was given to me, a messenger of Satan to buffet me . . . Concerning this thing I pleaded with the Lord three times that it might depart from me. And He said to me, "My grace is sufficient for you, for my strength is made perfect in weakness." Therefore most gladly I will rather boast in my infirmities, that the power of Christ may rest upon me. For when I am weak, then I am strong.

CHRIST CHURCH [PROTESTANT] | *Jerusalem, Israel*

ALL UNNECESSARY THINGS IN MY LIFE ARE PRUNED AWAY TILL I JUST KNOW JESUS

JOHN 15:5

"I am the vine, you are the branches. He who abides in Me, and I in him, bears much fruit; for without Me you can do nothing."

2 CORINTHIANS 7:1

Therefore, having these promises, beloved, let us cleanse ourselves from all filthiness of the flesh and spirit, perfecting holiness in the fear of God.

ISAIAH 48:10

"Behold, I have refined you, but not as silver; I have tested you in the furnace of affliction."

ROMANS 8:28

And we know that all things work together for good to those who love God, to those who are the called according to His purpose.

HOSEA 5:15B

"In their affliction, they will earnestly seek Me."

PSALM 91:15–16

"He shall call upon Me, and I will answer him; I will be with him in trouble; I will deliver him and honor him . . . and show him My salvation."

ROMANS 12:2

And do not be conformed to this world, but be transformed by the renewing of your mind, that you may prove what is that good and acceptable and perfect will of God.

JOHN 15:1–2

"I am the true vine, and My Father is the vinedresser. Every branch in Me that does not bear fruit He takes away; and every branch that bears fruit He prunes, that it may bear more fruit."

ROMANS 7:19, 24–25

For the good that I will to do, I do not do; but the evil I will not to do, that I practice. O wretched man that I am! Who will deliver me from this body of death? I thank God—through Jesus Christ our Lord! So then, with the mind I myself serve the law of God, but with the flesh the law of sin.

✠ Honor Thy Father and Thy Mother
That Thy Days May Be Long in the Land
Which the Lord Thy God Giveth Thee

CHRIST
EPISCOPAL
CHURCH
Luray, VA

I WILL HONOR AND RESPECT MY PARENTS

EPHESIANS 6:1–3

Children, obey your parents in the Lord, for this is right. "Honor your father and mother," which is the first commandment with promise: "That it may be well with you and you may live long on the earth."

COLOSSIANS 3:20–21
Children, obey your parents in all things, for this is well pleasing to the Lord. Fathers, do not provoke your children, lest they become discouraged.

LUKE 9:48
"Whoever receives this little child in My name receives Me; and whoever receives Me receives Him who sent Me."

PROVERBS 20:7
The righteous man walks in his integrity; his children are blessed after him.

PSALM 37:25
I have been young, and now am old; yet I have not seen the righteous forsaken, nor his descendants begging bread.

I WILL LOVE, INSTRUCT, CORRECT, AND TRAIN MY CHILDREN

PSALM 127:3–5A
Behold, children are a heritage from the LORD, the fruit of the womb is a reward. Like arrows in the hand of a warrior, so are the children of one's youth. Happy is the man who has his quiver full of them.

PROVERBS 1:8
My son, hear the instruction of your father, and do not forsake the law of your mother.

PROVERBS 29:17
Correct your son, and he will give you rest; yes, he will give delight to your soul.

ST. JAMES'S EPISCOPAL CHURCH | *Richmond, VA*

PROVERBS 22:6
Train up a child in the way he should go, and when he is old he will not depart from it.

PROVERBS 17:6
Children's children are the crown of old men, and the glory of children is their father.

MARK 10:14B, 16
"Let the little children come to Me." And He took them up in His arms . . . and blessed them.

JESUS WILL HELP US HONOR EACH OTHER AS PARTNERS

GENESIS 2:18

And the LORD God said, "It is not good that man should be alone; I will make him a helper comparable to him."

PROVERBS 31:10–11A, 28, 30

Who can find a virtuous wife? For her worth is far above rubies. The heart of her husband safely trusts her. Her children rise up and call her blessed; her husband also, and he praises her. Charm is deceitful and beauty is passing, but a woman who fears the LORD, she shall be praised.

SONG OF SOLOMON 1:15, 16A; 2:16A

Behold, you are fair, my love! Behold, you are fair! You have dove's eyes.

Behold, you are handsome, my beloved! Yes, pleasant! My beloved is mine, and I am his.

1 PETER 3:1, 7; & EPHESIANS 5:28

Wives, likewise, be submissive to your own husbands, that even if some do not obey the word, they, without a word, may be won by the conduct of their wives. Husbands, likewise, dwell with them with understanding, giving honor to the wife . . . that your prayers may not be hindered. So husbands ought to love their own wives as their own bodies; he who loves his wife loves himself.

EPIPHANY PARISH IN GEORGETOWN [CATHOLIC]
Washington, D.C.

MARRIAGE IS A COVENANT RELATIONSHIP THAT GOD ORDAINED

MATTHEW 19:3–6

The Pharisees also came to Him, testing Him, and saying to Him, "Is it lawful for a man to divorce his wife for just any reason?" And He answered and said to them, "Have you not read that He who made them at the beginning 'made them male and female,' and said, 'For this reason a man shall leave his father and mother and be joined to his wife, and the two shall become one flesh?' So then, they are no longer two but one flesh. Therefore what God has joined together, let not man separate."

PROVERBS 5:15A, 18B–19

Drink water from your own cistern . . . rejoice with the wife of your youth. As a loving deer and a graceful doe, let her breasts satisfy you at all times; and always be enraptured with her love.

PHILIPPIANS 2:14

Do all things without complaining and disputing.

EPHESIANS 4:31–32

Let all bitterness, wrath, anger, clamor, and evil speaking be put away from you, with all malice. And be kind to one another, tenderhearted, forgiving one another, even as God in Christ forgave you.

THE EVANGELICAL
LUTHERAN
CHURCH
Frederick, MD

LIVING IN THE HEART OF GOD IS LIVING A LIFE OF PRAYER AND FELLOWSHIP WITH HIM

1 THESSALONIANS 5:17; MARK 11:24

Pray without ceasing . . . "Therefore I say to you, whatever things you ask when you pray, believe that you receive them, and you will have them."

MATTHEW 6:6A, 8B; 7:7–8

"But you, when you pray, go into your room, and when you have shut your door, pray to your Father who is in the secret place . . . For your Father knows the things you have need of before you ask Him. Ask, and it will be given to you; seek, and you will find; knock, and it will be opened to you. For everyone who asks receives, and he who seeks finds, and to him who knocks it will be opened."

ROMANS 8:26

Likewise the Spirit also helps in our weaknesses. For we do not know what we should pray for as we ought, but the Spirit Himself makes intercession for us with groanings which cannot be uttered.

PSALM 122:6

Pray for the peace of Jerusalem: "May they prosper who love you."

I PRAY THAT MY HEART WILL BE FILLED WITH THE FAITH, HOPE, AND LOVE OF JESUS

LUKE 12:22A, 31A, 32, 34

He said to His disciples, "But seek the kingdom of God . . . Do not fear, little flock, for it is your Father's good pleasure to give you the kingdom. For where your treasure is, there your heart will be also."

SAINT ANNE'S EPISCOPAL CHURCH | *Annapolis, MD*

HEBREWS 11:1

Now faith is the substance of things hoped for, the evidence of things not seen.

JEREMIAH 17:7

"Blessed is the man who trusts in the LORD, and whose hope is the LORD."

1 CORINTHIANS 13:13

And now abide faith, hope, love, these three; but the greatest of these is love.

JOHN 13:34A

"A new commandment I give to you, that you love one another, as I have loved you . . ."

Blessed are the pure in heart for they shall see GOD

SAINT THOMAS'
EPISCOPAL CHURCH
Orange, VA

"Blessed are the pure in heart,
for they shall see God."

TRINITY
LUTHERAN
CHURCH
Hagerstown, MD

From the Old to the New World

THE CHRISTIAN LIFE: SERVICE TO SANCTIFICATION

JESUS, JESUS, SPEAK TO ME FOR I AM LISTENING AND WANT TO KNOW YOU MORE

LIFE IS A BATTLE, BUT IF I LOVE JESUS, I AM IN THE RANKS AND WILL FOLLOW HIM

ISAIAH 6:8
Also I heard the voice of the Lord, saying, "Whom shall I send, and who will go for Us?" Then I said, "Here am I! Send me."

2 TIMOTHY 1:7
For God has not given us a spirit of fear, but of power and of love and of a sound mind.

JOHN 21:15
Jesus said to Simon Peter, "Simon . . . do you love Me more than these? . . . Feed My lambs."

MARK 6:7, 12–13
And He called the twelve to Himself, and began to send them out two by two, and gave them power over unclean spirits. So they went out and preached that people should repent. And they cast out many demons, and anointed with oil many who were sick, and healed them.

MATTHEW 10:16
"Behold, I send you out as sheep in the midst of wolves. Therefore be wise as serpents and harmless as doves."

MATTHEW 17:5

Behold, a bright cloud overshadowed them; and suddenly a voice came out of the cloud, saying, "This is My beloved Son, in whom I am well pleased. Hear Him!"

JOHN 20:21–22
So Jesus said to them again, "Peace to you! As the Father has sent Me, I also send you." And when He had said this, He breathed on them, and said to them, "Receive the Holy Spirit."

THE EPISCOPAL
CHURCH OF
THE EPIPHANY
Danville, VA

CHRIST LUTHERAN CHURCH | *Washington, D.C.*
John 8:12, John 15:1, John 10:7, John 6:48

On the battlefield I need to have the whole armor of God to oppose Satan

I will keep my eyes fixed on the Lord, my banner and my commander-in-chief

JOSHUA 1:9

"Be strong and of good courage; do not be afraid, nor be dismayed, for the LORD your God is with you wherever you go."

MATTHEW 10:7–8

"And as you go, preach, saying, 'The kingdom of heaven is at hand.' Heal the sick, cleanse the lepers, raise the dead, cast out demons. Freely you have received, freely give."

LUKE 10:17–20

Then the seventy returned with joy, saying, "Lord, even the demons are subject to us in Your name." And He said to them, "I saw Satan fall like lightning from heaven. Behold, I give you the authority to trample on serpents and scorpions, and over all the power of the enemy, and nothing shall by any means hurt you. Nevertheless do not rejoice in this, that the spirits are subject to you, but rather rejoice because your names are written in heaven."

PSALM 60:12

Through God we will do valiantly, for it is He who shall tread down our enemies.

ST. MICHAEL'S EPISCOPAL CHURCH | *Arlington, VA*

EPHESIANS 6:10–18

Finally, my brethren, be strong in the Lord and in the power of His might. Put on the whole armor of God, that you may be able to stand against the wiles of the devil. For we do not wrestle against flesh and blood, but against principalities, against powers, against the rulers of the darkness of this age, against spiritual hosts of wickedness in the heavenly places. Therefore take up the whole armor of God, that you may be able to withstand in the evil day, and having done all, to stand. Stand therefore, having girded your waist with truth, having put on the breastplate of righteousness, and having shod your feet with the preparation of the gospel of peace; above all, taking the shield of faith with which you will be able to quench all the fiery darts of the wicked one. And take the helmet of salvation, and the sword of the Spirit, which is the word of God; praying always with all prayer and supplication in the Spirit, being watchful to this end with all perseverance and supplication for all the saints.

THE WORD OF THE LORD HAS GONE FORTH AND I WILL HELP WITH THE HARVEST

I DO UNDERSTAND THAT SERVING MY CREATOR IS ABOUT SACRIFICE FOR HIS GLORY

MICAH 6:8
And what does the LORD require of you but to do justly, to love mercy, and to walk humbly with your God?

ROMANS 12:1
I beseech you therefore, brethren, by the mercies of God, that you present your bodies a living sacrifice, holy, acceptable to God, which is your reasonable service.

ST. STEPHEN'S EPISCOPAL CHURCH | *Catlett, VA*

JOHN 15:13
"Greater love has no one than this, than to lay down one's life for his friends."

COLOSSIANS 1:24; 1 THESSALONIANS 2:7–8
I now rejoice in my sufferings for you, and fill up in my flesh what is lacking in the afflictions of Christ, for the sake of His body, which is the church . . . But we were gentle among you, just as a nursing mother cherishes her own children. So, affectionately longing for you, we were well pleased to impart to you not only the gospel of God, but also our own lives, because you had become dear to us.

LUKE 10:2
Then He said to them, "The harvest truly is great, but the laborers are few; therefore pray the Lord of the harvest to send out laborers into His harvest."

REVELATION 14:14–16
Then I looked, and behold, a white cloud, and on the cloud sat One like the Son of Man, having on His head a golden crown, and in His hand a sharp sickle. And another angel came out of the temple, crying with a loud voice to Him who sat on the cloud, "Thrust in Your sickle and reap, for the time has come for You to reap, for the harvest of the earth is ripe." So He who sat on the cloud thrust in His sickle on the earth, and the earth was reaped.

HOSEA 4:6A
"My people are destroyed for lack of knowledge."

PSALM 27:14
Wait on the LORD; be of good courage, and He shall strengthen your heart; wait, I say, on the LORD!

Dear Lord, Being with you is more precious to me than life on earth

I am a joyful bondservant in the service of my Lord Jesus Christ

PHILIPPIANS 3:8; 1:21
Yet indeed I also count all things loss for the excellence of the knowledge of Christ Jesus my Lord, for whom I have suffered the loss of all things, and count them as rubbish, that I may gain Christ. For to me, to live is Christ, and to die is gain.

PHILIPPIANS 2:5, 7–8
Let this mind be in you which was also in Christ Jesus, who . . . made Himself of no reputation, taking the form of a bondservant, and coming in the likeness of men. And being found in appearance as a man, He humbled Himself and became obedient to the point of death, even the death of the cross.

1 CORINTHIANS 9:19; 7:22–23
For though I am free from all men, I have made myself a servant to all, that I might win the more. For he who is called in the Lord . . . while free is Christ's slave. You were bought at a price; do not become slaves of men.

HEBREWS 12:1–2
Therefore we also, since we are surrounded by so great a cloud of witnesses, let us lay aside every weight, and the sin which so easily ensnares us, and let us run with endurance the race that is set before us, looking unto Jesus, the author and finisher of our faith, who for the joy that was set before Him endured the cross, despising the shame, and has sat down at the right hand of the throne of God.

REVELATION 12:10B–11
For the accuser . . . has been cast down. And they overcame him by the blood of the Lamb and by the word of their testimony, and they did not love their lives to the death.

PSALM 116:15
Precious in the sight of the LORD is the death of His saints.

Servus Domini

ST. PETER EN GALLICANTU
Jerusalem, Israel

CHAPEL AT THE
UNIVERSITY OF
VIRGINIA
Charlottesville, VA

LORD, WHEN I TELL OTHERS ABOUT YOU, HELP THEM TO SEE WHO YOU ARE

YOU, JESUS, PRAY FOR US; I PRAY FOR OTHERS AND FOR THOSE IN AUTHORITY

REVELATION 5:8

The four living creatures and the twenty-four elders [in heaven] fell down before the Lamb, each having a harp, and golden bowls full of incense, which are the prayers of the saints.

JOHN 17:20–21

"I do not pray for these alone, but also for those who will believe in Me through their word; that they all may be one, as You, Father, are in Me, and I in You; that they also may be one in Us."

2 CHRONICLES 7:14

"If My people who are called by My name will humble themselves, and pray and seek My face, and turn from their wicked ways, then I will hear from heaven, and forgive their sin and heal their land."

ROMANS 1:1; 1 TIMOTHY 2: 1–6

Paul, a bondservant of Jesus Christ, called to be an apostle, separated to the gospel of God . . . exhort: that supplications, prayers, intercessions, and giving of thanks be made from all men, for kings and all who are in authority, that we may lead a quiet and peaceable life in all godliness and reverence. For this is good and acceptable in the sight of God our savior, who desires all men to be saved and to come to the knowledge of the truth. For there is one God and one Mediator between God and men, the Man Christ Jesus, who gave Himself a ransom for all.

MARK 16:15–18

And He said to them, "Go into all the world and preach the gospel to every creature. He who believes and is baptized will be saved; but he who does not believe will be condemned. And these signs will follow those who believe: In My name they will cast out demons; they will speak with new tongues; they will take up serpents; and if they drink anything deadly, it will by no means hurt them; they will lay hands on the sick, and they will recover."

1 CORINTHIANS 1:23–24

We preach Christ crucified, to the Jews a stumbling block and to the Greeks foolishness, but to those who are called . . . Christ the power of God and the wisdom of God.

MARK 5:19

"Go home to your friends, and tell them what great things the Lord has done for you, and how He has had compassion on you."

ST. MARY'S EPISCOPAL CHURCH
Washington, D.C

BLESSED ARE THE MERCIFUL FOR THEY SHALL OBTAIN MERCY—

JAMES 1:27

YES LORD, I SEE YOU IN THE POOR AS I SERVE THEM. DO THEY SEE YOU IN ME?

PROVERBS 19:17
He who has pity on the poor lends to the LORD, and He will pay back what He has given.

ROMANS 15:1–2
We then who are strong ought to bear with the scruples of the weak, and not to please ourselves. Let each of us please his neighbor for his good, leading to edification.

MATTHEW 25:31–34, 41A, 46, 40
"When the Son of Man comes in His glory, and all the holy angels with Him, then He will sit on the throne of His glory. All the nations will be gathered before Him, and He will separate them one from another, as a shepherd divides his sheep from the goats. And He will set the sheep on His right hand, but the goats on the left. Then the King will say to those on His right hand, 'Come, you blessed of My Father, inherit the kingdom prepared for you . . .' Then He will also say to those on the left hand, 'Depart from me.' And these will go away into everlasting punishment, but the righteous into eternal life.

Pure and undefiled religion before God and the Father is this: to visit orphans and widows in their trouble, and to keep oneself unspotted from the world.

MATTHEW 5:7
Blessed are the merciful, for they shall obtain mercy.

MATTHEW 25:37-39
Then the righteous will answer Him, saying, "Lord, when did we see You hungry and feed You, or thirsty and give You drink? When did we see You a stranger and take You in, or naked and clothe You? Or when did we see You sick, or in prison, and come to You?" And the King will answer and say to them, "Assuredly, I say to you, inasmuch as you did it to one of the least of these My brethren, you did it to Me."

EMMANUEL CHURCH AT BROOK HILL
Richmond, VA

a stranger and take You in

see You hungry and feed You

see You sick

THE CHURCH OF THE EPIPHANY [EPISCOPAL] *Washington, D.C.*—two side windows
MEADE MEMORIAL EPISCOPAL CHURCH *Alexandria, VA*—center window

I WILL GIVE OTHERS THE LIVING WATER OF JESUS CHRIST

COMFORTING OTHERS WITH THE LOVE AND HEALING TOUCH OF THE LORD BLESSES ME

2 CORINTHIANS 1:3–4
Blessed be the God and Father of our Lord Jesus Christ, the Father of mercies and God of all comfort, who comforts us in all our tribulation, that we may be able to comfort those who are in any trouble, with the comfort with which we ourselves are comforted by God.

MATTHEW 5:4
"Blessed are those who mourn, for they shall be comforted."

ROMANS 8:18
For I consider that the sufferings of this present time are not worthy to be compared with the glory which shall be revealed in us.

1 JOHN 3:18
My little children, let us not love in word or in tongue, but in deed and in truth.

GALATIANS 6:9
And let us not grow weary while doing good, for in due season we shall reap if we do not lose heart.

MATTHEW 25:35B
"I was thirsty and you gave Me drink . . ."

ISAIAH 55:1A, 6
"Ho! Everyone who thirsts, come to the waters . . ." Seek the LORD while He may be found, call upon Him while He is near.

JOHN 4:10, 14A
Jesus answered and said to her, "If you knew the gift of God, and who it is who says to you, 'Give Me a drink,' you would have asked Him and He would have given you living water. Whoever drinks of the water that I shall give him will never thirst."

MARK 9:41
"For whoever gives you a cup of water to drink in My name, because you belong to Christ, assuredly, I say to you, he will by no means lose his reward."

ST. JAMES'S EPISCOPAL CHURCH
Richmond, VA

Finally, Live in Victory, for the Trumpet Will Sound and He Will Return!

Live Expectantly
Find Joy in the Presence of the Lord and Live as if He Would Come Tomorrow

PSALM 95:6
Oh come, let us worship and bow down; let us kneel before the Lord our Maker.

1 CORINTHIANS 15:57
Thanks be to God, who gives us the victory through our Lord Jesus Christ.

HEBREWS 10:23–25
Let us hold fast the confession of our hope without wavering, for He who promised is faithful. And let us consider one another in order to stir up love and good works, not forsaking the assembling of ourselves together, as in the manner of some, but exhorting one another, and so much the more as you see the Day approaching.

1 JOHN 2:28
And now, little children, abide in Him, that when He appears, we may have confidence and not be ashamed before Him at His coming.

JAMES 5:8
You also be patient. Establish your hearts, for the coming of the Lord is at hand.

ST. JAMES' EPISCOPAL CHURCH | *Warrenton, VA*

MARK 13:24, 26, 33
"But in those days, after that tribulation, the sun will be darkened . . . Then they will see the Son of Man coming in the clouds with great power and glory. Take heed, watch and pray; for you do not know when the time is."

REVELATION 22:12
"And behold, I am coming quickly, and My reward is with Me, to give every one according to his work."

1 THESSALONIANS 4:16–17
For the Lord Himself will descend from heaven with a shout, with the voice of an archangel, and with the trumpet of God. And the dead in Christ will rise first. Then we who are alive and remain shall be caught up together with them in the clouds to meet the Lord in the air.

PSALM 96:13
For He is coming, for He is coming to judge the earth. He shall judge the world with righteousness, and the peoples with His truth.

IN MEMORY OF J. WARREN HASTINGS 1897 1960

THE NATIONAL CITY
CHRISTIAN CHURCH
Washington, D.C.

AND PEACE WILL REIGN OVER ALL THE WORLD

AND MAN WILL BE RESTORED TO THE GARDEN OF EDEN

REVELATION 22:1–2, 5A

And He showed me a pure river of water of life, clear as crystal, proceeding from the throne of God and of the Lamb. In the middle of its street, and on either side of river, was the tree of life, which bore twelve fruits, each tree yielding its fruit every month. The leaves of the tree were for the healing of the nations. There shall be no night there: they need no lamp nor light of the sun, for the Lord God gives them light.

ISAIAH 51:3

The LORD will comfort all her waste places; He will make her wilderness like Eden, and her desert like the garden of the LORD; joy and gladness will be found in it, thanksgiving and the voice of melody.

PSALM 46:4A; REVELATION 22:17B

There is a river whose streams shall make glad the city of God. And let him who thirsts come. Whoever desires, let him take the water of life freely.

EMMANUEL CHAPEL, CUNNINGHAM CHAPEL PARISH [EPISCOPAL] | *Boyce, VA*

ISAIAH 11:3B–6

He shall not judge by the sight of His eyes, nor decide by the hearing of His ears; but with righteousness He shall judge the poor, and decide with equity for the meek of the earth; He shall strike the earth with the rod of His mouth, and with the breath of His lips He shall slay the wicked. Righteousness shall be the belt of His loins, and faithfulness the belt of His waist. The wolf also shall dwell with the lamb, the leopard shall lie down with the young goat, the calf and the young lion and the fattling together; and a little child shall lead them.

John has a vision of a new world

REVELATION 21:1–7

The Devil is destroyed

REVELATION 20:1A, 2–3A, 7–10

Then I saw an angel coming down from heaven. He laid hold of the dragon, that serpent of old, who is the Devil and Satan, and bound him for a thousand years; and he cast him into the bottomless pit . . . Now when the thousand years have expired, Satan will be released from his prison and will go out to deceive the nations which are in the four corners of the earth, Gog and Magog, to gather them together to battle, whose number is as the sand of the sea. They went up on the breadth of the earth and surrounded the camp of the saints and the beloved city. And fire came down from God out of heaven and devoured them. The devil, who deceived them, was cast into the lake of fire and brimstone . . . and they will be tormented day and night forever and ever.

Now I saw a new heaven and a new earth, for the first heaven and the first earth had passed away. Also there was no more sea. Then I, John, saw the holy city, New Jerusalem, coming down out of heaven from God, prepared as a bride adorned for her husband. And I heard a loud voice from heaven saying, "Behold, the tabernacle of God is with men, and He will dwell with them, and they shall be His people. God Himself will be with them and be their God. And God will wipe away every tear from their eyes; there shall be no more death, nor sorrow, nor crying. There shall be no more pain, for the former things have passed away." Then He who sat on the throne said, "Behold, I make all things new." And He said to me. "It is done! I am the Alpha and the Omega, the Beginning and the End. I will give of the fountain of the water of life freely to him who thirsts. He who overcomes shall inherit all things, and I will be his God and he shall be My son."

SAINT THOMAS' EPISCOPAL CHURCH
Orange, VA

ST. JAMES'
EPISCOPAL
CHURCH
Warrenton, VA

JESUS, THE LAMB OF GOD, IS THE LIGHT OF THIS HEAVENLY CITY FOR THE REDEEMED

ONLY JESUS IS WORTHY TO OPEN THE SEALS TO THE FATE OF THE WORLD

REVELATION 5:8–10, 13B
Now when He had taken the scroll, the four living creatures and the twenty-four elders fell down before the Lamb, each having a harp, and golden bowls full of incense,

ST. JOHN'S EPISCOPAL CHURCH, LAFAYETTE SQUARE | *Washington, D.C.*

which are the prayers of the saints. And they sang a new song, saying: "You are worthy to take the scroll, and to open its seals; for You were slain, and have redeemed us to God by Your blood out of every tribe and tongue and people and nation, and have made us kings and priests to our God; and we shall reign on the earth. Blessing and honor and glory and power be to Him who sits on the throne, and to the Lamb, forever and ever!"

REVELATION 21:22–25, 27

But I saw no temple in it, for the Lord God Almighty and the Lamb are its temple. The city had no need of the sun or of the moon to shine in it, for the glory of God illuminated it. The Lamb is its light. And the nations of those who are saved shall walk in its light, and the kings of the earth bring their glory and honor into it. Its gates shall not be shut at all by day (there shall be no night there). But there shall by no means enter it anything that defiles, or causes an abomination or a lie, but only those who are written in the Lamb's Book of Life.

ISAIAH 51:11
So shall the ransomed of the LORD shall return, and come to Zion with singing, with everlasting joy on their heads. They shall obtain joy and gladness; sorrow and sighing shall flee away.

YOU ARE VICTORIOUS AND AWESOME, DEAR LORD!

JOHN 16:33B; REVELATION 1:8, 18A, 3:5

WHO CAN BUT COME TO YOU BUT TO FALL DOWN AND WORSHIP BEFORE YOU?

ISAIAH 66:18B, 20A

"It shall be that I will gather all nations and tongues; and they shall come and see My glory. Then they shall bring all your brethren for an offering to the LORD out of all nations, on horses and in chariots and in litters, on mules and on camels, to My holy mountain Jerusalem," says the LORD.

JEREMIAH 3:17

"At that time Jerusalem shall be called The Throne of the LORD, and all the nations shall be gathered to it, to the name of the LORD, to Jerusalem. No more shall they follow the dictates of their evil hearts."

REVELATION 15:3–4A

They sing the song of Moses, the servant of God, and the song of the Lamb, saying: "Great and marvelous are Your works, Lord God Almighty! Just and true are Your ways, O King of the saints! Who shall not fear You, O Lord, and glorify Your name? For You alone are holy. For all nations shall come and worship before You."

ALL SAINTS EPISCOPAL CHURCH | *Chevy Chase, MD*

" I have overcome the world. I am the Alpha and the Omega, the Beginning and the End," says the LORD, "who is and who was and who is to come, the Almighty. I am He who lives, and was dead, and behold, I am alive forevermore. Amen. He who overcomes shall be clothed in white garments, and I will not blot out his name from the Book of Life; but I will confess his name before My Father and before His angels."

REVELATION 1:13–17

I saw . . . One like the Son of Man, clothed with a garment down to the feet and girded about the chest with a golden band. His head and hair were white like wool, as white as snow, and His eyes like a flame of fire; His feet were like fine brass, as if refined in a furnace, and His voice as the sound of many waters; He had in His right hand seven stars, out of His mouth went a sharp two-edged sword, and His countenance was like the sun shining in its strength. And when I saw Him, I fell at His feet as dead. But He laid his right hand on me, saying to me, "Do not be afraid; I am the First and the Last."

OUR GOD IS WORTHY OF PRAISE FROM GRATEFUL HEARTS!

LORD, HELP ME TO BE COURAGEOUS AND FAITHFUL TO THE END

JAMES 1:12

Blessed is the man who endures temptation; for when he has been approved, he will receive the crown of life which the Lord has promised to those who love Him.

REVELATION 2:2A, 3, 10B

"I know your works, your labor, your patience, and that you cannot bear those who are evil . . . and you have persevered and have patience, and have labored for My name's sake and have not become weary. Be faithful until death, and I will give you the crown of life."

REVELATION 3:21

"To him who overcomes I will grant to sit with Me on My throne, as I also overcame and sat down with My Father on His throne."

MATTHEW 25:6B; REVELATION 22:17A

"'Behold, the bridegroom is coming; go out to meet him!'" And the Spirit and the bride say, "Come!" And let him who hears say, "Come!"

MATTHEW 25:21; JOHN 14:27

"Well done, good and faithful servant . . . Enter into the joy of your Lord. Peace I leave with you, My peace I give to you; not as the world gives do I give to you. Let not your heart be troubled, neither let it be afraid."

CHRIST CHURCH, GEORGETOWN [EPISCOPAL] *Washington, D.C.*

PSALM 100: 4–4

Enter into His gates with thanksgiving, and into His courts with praise. Be thankful to Him, and bless His name. For the LORD is good; His mercy is everlasting, and His truth endures to all generations.

PSALM 84:2

My soul longs, yes, even faints for the courts of the LORD; my heart and my flesh cry out for the living God.

PSALM 30:11

You have turned for me my mourning into dancing; you have put off my sackcloth and clothed me with gladness.

PSALM 92:1–2

It is good to give thanks to the LORD, and to sing praises to Your name, O Most High; to declare Your lovingkindness in the morning, and Your faithfulness every night.

PSALM 37:4

Delight yourself also in the LORD, and He shall give you the desires of your heart.

PHILIPPIANS 4:4

Rejoice in the LORD always. Again I will say, rejoice!

ENTER INTO HIS GATES
WITH THANKS GIVING

CHRIST
EPISCOPAL
CHURCH
Charlottesville, VA

OF SUCH IS THE
KINGDOM OF
HEAVEN

THE END...
OR YOUR BEGINNING?

Dear Father God, I come to you as a sinner and ask that you forgive me. I want to be born into your kingdom as you have promised those who ask. I believe that Jesus Christ is your Son, lived on the earth, and died for me, paying for my sins, but rose to rule with you in heaven. Through the cross, I pray that you would come and live in my heart and be Lord of my life. I surrender my life to you and look forward to your Holy Spirit teaching, guiding, cleansing, and giving me your joy. I want to have victory in my life over my problems, pain, and wounds.

Thank you for my life, Father. I love You.

Your child

CHRIST EPISCOPAL
CHURCH
Charlottesville, VA

I am the way, the truth, and the life. No one comes to the Father except through Me. "

"Nevertheless I tell you the truth, it is to your advantage that I go away; for if I do not go away, the Helper will not come to you. However, when He, the Spirit of truth has come, He will guide you into all truth, for He will not speak on His own authority, but whatever He hears He will speak; and He will tell you of things to come. He will glorify Me, for He will take what is Mine and declare it to you."

JOHN 14:27

"Peace I leave with you, My peace I give to you; not as the world gives do I give to you. Let not your heart be troubled, neither let it be afraid."

"I am the Alpha and the Omega,
the Beginning and the End."